Python Programming for Beginners

A 7 Days Practical Guide to Fast Learn Python Programming and Coding Language (with Exercises)

By James Deep

professional before attempting any techniques outlined in this book.

By reading this document, the reader agrees that under no circumstances is the author responsible for any losses, direct or indirect, which are incurred as a result of the use of information contained within this document, including, but not limited to, — errors, omissions, or inaccuracies.

Table of Contents

Introduction

In this Python Beginner's guide, you're about to learn:

- The Most Vital Basics of Python programming. Rapidly get the dialect and begin applying the ideas to any code that you compose.
- The Useful features of Python for Beginners-including some ideas you can apply to in real-world situations and even other programs.
- Different mechanics of Python programming: control stream, factors, records/lexicons, and classes-and why taking in these center standards are essential to Python achievement
- Protest arranged programming, its impact on present-day scripting languages, and why it makes a difference.

This book has been composed specifically for Newbies and Beginners. You will be taken through each step of your very first program, and we will explain each portion of the script as you test and analyze the data.

In common computing programs, formulas are groups of individually programmed orders that are used by computers to determine outcomes and solve problems. Instead, machine learning formulas allow computers to focus only on data that is inputted and use proven stat analysis in order to deliver correct values that fall within a certain probability. What this means is that computers have the ability to break down simple data models which enables it to automate routine decision-making steps based on the specific data that was inputted.

There are many books about Python Programming on the market. Thank you so much for selecting this one! Be assured that every measure was put in place to see to it that this book contains much useful details as possible, please enjoy reading the book!

FIRST DAY

Part 1: Introduction

Python is an awesome decision on machine learning for a few reasons. Most importantly, it's a basic dialect at first glance. Regardless of whether you're not acquainted with Python, getting up to speed is snappy in the event that you at any point have utilized some other dialect with C-like grammar.

Second, Python has an incredible network which results in great documentation and inviting and extensive answers in Stack Overflow (central!).

Third, coming from the colossal network, there are a lot of valuable libraries for Python (both as "batteries included" an outsider), which take care of essentially any issue that you can have (counting machine learning).

History of Python

Python was invented in the later years of the 1980s. Guido van Rossum, the founder, started using the language in December 1989. He is Python's only known creator and his integral role in the growth and development of the language has earned him the nickname "Benevolent Dictator for Life". It was created to be the successor to the language known as ABC.

The next version that was released was Python 2.0, in October of the year 2000 and had significant upgrades and new highlights, including a cycle- distinguishing junk jockey and back up support for Unicode. It was most fortunate, that this particular version, made vast improvement procedures to the language turned out to be more straightforward and network sponsored.

Python 3.0, which initially started its existence as Py3K. This version was rolled out in December of 2008 after a rigorous testing period. This particular version of Python was hard to roll back to previous compatible versions which are the most unfortunate. Yet, a significant number of its real highlights have been rolled back to versions 2.6 or 2.7 (Python), and rollouts of Python 3 which utilizes the two to three utilities, that helps to automate the interpretation of the Python script.

Python 2.7's expiry date was originally supposed to be back in 2015, but for unidentifiable reasons, it was put off until the year 2020. It was known that there was a major concern about data being unable to roll back but roll FORWARD into the new version, Python 3. In 2017, Google declared that there would be work done on Python 2.7 to enhance execution under simultaneously running tasks.

Basic Features of Python

Python is an unmistakable and extremely robust programming language that is object-oriented based almost identical to Ruby, Perl, and Java, A portion of Python's remarkable highlights:

- Python uses a rich structure, influencing, and composing projects that can be analyzed simpler.
- It accompanies a huge standard library that backs tons of simple programming commands, for example, extremely seamless web server connections, processing and handling files, and the ability to search through text with commonly used expressions and commands.

- Python's easy to use interactive interface makes it simple to test shorter pieces of coding. It also comes with IDLE which is a "development environment".

Common Programming Language Features of Python

I. A huge array of common data types: floating point numbers, complex numbers, infinite length integers, ASCII strings, and Unicode, as well as a large variety of dictionaries and lists.

II. Python is guided in an object-oriented framework, with multiple classes and inheritance.

III. Python code can be bundled together into different modules and packages.

Python is notorious for being a much cleaner language for error handling due to

the catching and raising of exceptions allowed.

IV. Information is firmly and progressively composed. Blending incongruent data types, for example, adding a string and a number together, raises an exception right away where errors are caught significantly sooner than later.

V.   Python has advanced coding highlights such as comprehending lists and iterators.

Summary

- Python effortlessly extended out by including new modules executed in a source code like C or C++.
- Python can also be inserted into another application to give an easily programmed interface.
- Python will run anyplace, including OS X, Windows Environment, Linux, and even UNIX, with informal models for the Android and iOS environments.
- Python can easily be recorded, modified and re-downloaded and distributed, be unreservedly adjusted and re-disseminated. While it is copyrighted, it's accessible under open source.
- Ultimately, Python is available free of charge.

Part 2: Installing Python

Python is both procedural and object-oriented coding language. It has an easy syntax. Python programming language is cross-platform implying that it can be run on different Operating Systems environments such as Linux, Windows platform, Mac OS X platform, UNIX platform and can be ported to .NET and Java virtual machines. Python programming language is free and open source. While most recent versions of Mac and Linux have Python preinstalled, it is recommended that one installs and runs the current version.

Installing Python

Most recent versions of Linux and Mac have Python already installed in them. However, you might need to install Python and the following are the steps for installing Python in Windows, Mac OS X or Linux.

Installing Python in Macintosh Operating System X

I. Visit Download Python page which is the credible site and click "Download Python 3.7.2 (The version may differ from the one stated here).

II. When the download completes, click open the package and follow the instructions given. The installation should complete with "The installation was successful" prompt.

III. Now, visit Download Notepad++ and download the text editor and install it by opening the package and following the message prompts. The Notepad++ text editor is free and suited to help write source code (raw text programming words).

Installing Python in Linux

It is now time to issue instructions to run the source code on your OS (Operating System)

Installing in Windows

I.   Visit Download Python site which is the recommended site and click "Download Python 3.7.2 (The version may differ from the one stated here).

II. When your download completes, open the package by clicking and follow the guidelines given. The Python installation should complete with "The installation was successful" prompt. When you install Python successfully, it also installs a program known as IDLE along it. IDLE is a graphical user interface when working with Python.

III. Now, visit Download Notepad++ and download the text editor and install it by opening the package and following the message prompts. The Notepad++ text editor is free and suited to help write source code (raw text programming words).

Modes of Running Python

Now before we start running our first python program it is important that we understand the ways in which we can run python programs. Running or executing or deploying or firing a program simply means that we making the computer process instructions/lines of codes. For instance, if the lines of codes (program) require the computer to display some message then it should. The following are the ways or mode of running python programs. The interpreter is a special program that is installed when installing the Python package and helps convert text code into a language that the computer understands and can act on it (executing).

I.   Immediate Mode

It is a way of running python programs that are not written in a file. We get into the immediate mode by typing the word python in the command line and which will trigger the interpreter to switch to immediate mode. The immediate mode allows typing of expressions directly and pressing enter generates the output. The sign below is the Python prompt:

>>>

The python prompt instructs the interpreter to accept input from the user. For instance, typing 2+2 and pressing enter will display 4 as the output. In a way, this prompt can be used as a calculator. If you need to exit the immediate mode, type quit() or exit().

Now type 5 +3, and press enter, the output should be 8. The next mode is the Script Mode.

II.   Script Mode

The script mode is used to run a python program written in a file, the file is called a script.

The scripts can be saved to external storage such as a disk for later use. All python scripts have the file extension .py which implies that the filename ends with .py. An example is myFirstProg.py. We shall explain later how to write python scripts.

Integrated Development Environment (IDE)

An IDE provides a convenient way of writing and running Python programs. One can also use text editors to create a python script file instead of an IDE by writing lines of codes and saving the file with a .py extension. However, using an IDE can simplify the process of writing and running Python programs. The IDEL present in the Python package is an example of an IDE with a graphical user interface and gets installed along the Python language. The advantages of IDE include helping getting rid of repetitive tasks and simplify coding for beginners. IDE provides syntax highlighting, code hinting, and syntax checking among other features. There also commercial IDE such as the PyScripter IDE that performs most of the mentioned functions.

Note:

We have presented what is Python programming language, how to download and install Python, the immediate and script modes of Python IDE, and what is an IDE.

Summary

- Python can be obtained from the **Python Software Foundation** website at python.org. Typically, that involves downloading the appropriate **installer** for your operating system and running it on your machine.
- Some operating systems, notably Linux, provide a **package manager** that can be run to install Python.
- On macOS, the best way to install Python 3 involves installing a package manager called **Homebrew**. You'll see how to do this in the relevant section in the tutorial.

Part 3: Variables

First Program in Python

The rest of illustrations will assume you are running the python programs in a Windows environment.

I.   Start IDLE

II.   Navigate to the File menu and click New Window

III. Type the following: print ("Hello World!")

IV.   On the file, menu click Save. Type the name of myProgram1.py

V.   Navigate to Run and click Run Module to run the program.

The first program that we have written is known as the "Hello World!" and is used to not only provide an introduction to a new computer coding language but also test the basic configuration of the IDE. The output of the program is "Hello World!" Here is what has happened, the Print() is an inbuilt function, it is prewritten and preloaded for you, is used to display whatever is contained in the () as long as it is between the double quotes. The computer will display anything written within the double quotes.

Practice Exercise: Now write and run the following python programs:

- ✓ print("I am now a Python Language Coder!")

- ✓   print("This is my second simple program!")

- ✓ print("I love the simplicity of Python")

- ✓ print("I will display whatever is here in quotes such as owyhen2589gdbnz082")

Now we need to write a program with numbers but before writing such a program we need to learn something about Variables and Types.

Remember python is object-oriented and it is not statically typed which means we do not need to declare variables before using them or specify their type. Let us explain this statement, an object-oriented language simply means that the language supports viewing and manipulating real-life scenarios as groups with subgroups that can be linked and shared mimicking the natural order and interaction of things. Not all programming languages are object oriented, for instance, Visual C programming language is not object-oriented. In programming, declaring variables means that we explicitly state the nature of the variable. The variable can be declared as an integer, long integer, short integer, floating integer, a string, or as a character including if it is accessible locally or globally. A variable is a storage location that changes values depending on conditions.

For instance, number1 can take any number from 0 to infinity. However, if we specify explicitly that int number1 it then means that the storage location will only accept integers and not fractions for instance. Fortunately or unfortunately, python does not require us to explicitly state the nature of the storage location (declare variables) as that is left to the python language itself to figure out that.

Before tackling types of variables and rules of writing variables, let us run a simple program to understand what variables when coding a python program are.

✓ Start IDLE

✓ Navigate to the File menu and click New Window

✓ Type the following:

num1=4

num2=5

sum=num1+num2

print(sum)

✓ On the file, menu click Save. Type the name of myProgram2.py

✓ Navigate to Run and click Run Module to run the program.

The expected output of this program should be "9" without the double quotes.

Discussion

At this point, you are eager to understand what has just happened and why the print(sum) does not have double quotes like the first programs we wrote. Here is the explanation.

The first line num1=4 means that variable num1(our shortened way of writing number1, first number) has been assigned 4 before the program runs.

The second line num2=5 means that variable num2(our shortened way of writing number2, second number) has been assigned 5 before the program runs.

The computer interprets these instructions and stores the numbers given

The third line sum=num1+num2 tells the computer that takes whatever num1 has been given and add to whatever num2 has been given. In other terms, sum the values of num1 and num2.

The fourth line print(sum) means that display whatever sum has. If we put double quotes to sum, the computer will simply display the word sum and not the sum of the two numbers! Remember that cliché that computers are garbage in and garbage out. They follow what you give them!

Note: + is an operator for summing variables and has other users that will be discussed later.

Now let us try out three exercises involving numbers before we explain types of variables and rules of writing variables so that you get more freedom to play with variables. Remember variables values vary for instance num1 can take 3, 8, 1562, 1.

Follow the steps of opening Python IDE and do the following:

- ✓ The output should be 54

num1=43

num2=11

sum=num1+num2

print(sum)

- ✓ The output should be 167

num1=101

num2=66

sum=num1+num2

print(sum)

- ✓ The output should be 28

num1=9

num2=19

sum=num1+num2

print(sum)

Variables

We have used num1, num2, and sum and the variable names were not just random, they must follow certain rules and conventions. Rules are what we cannot violate while conventions are much like the recommended way. Let us start with the rules:

The Rules of When Naming Variables in Python

I.   Variable names should always start with a letter or an underscore, i.e.

num1

_num1

II.   The remaining part of the variable name may consist of numbers, letters, and underscores, i.e.

number1

num_be_r

III.   Variable names are case sensitive meaning that capital letters and non-capital letters are treated differently.

Num1 will be treated differently with num1.

Practice Exercise

Write/suggest five variables for:

- ✓ Hospital department.

- ✓ Bank.

- ✓ Media House.

  Given scri=75, scr4=9, sscr2=13, Scr=18

- ✓ The variable names in above are supposed to represents scores of students. Rewrite the variables to satisfy Python variable rules and conventions.

Conventions When Naming Variables in Python

As earlier indicated, conventions are not rules per se are the established traditions that add value and readability to the way we name variables in Python.

- ❖ Uphold readability. Your variables should give a hint of what they are handling because programs are meant to be read by other people other than the person writing them.

number1 is easy to read compared to n1. Similarly, first_name is easy to read compared to firstname or firstName or fn. The implication of all these is that both are valid/acceptable variables in python but the convention is forcing us to write them in an easy to read form.

❖ Use descriptive names when writing your variables. For instance, number1 as a variable name is descriptive compared yale or mything. In other words, we can write yale to capture values for number1 but the name does not outrightly hint what we are doing. Remember when writing programs; assume another person will maintain them. The person should be able to quickly figure out what the program is all about before running it.

❖ Due to confusion, avoid using the uppercase 'O', lowercase letter 'l' and the uppercase letter 'I' because they can be confused with numbers. In other terms, using these letters will not be a violation of writing variables but their inclusion as variable names will breed confusion.

Practice Exercise 1

Re-write the following variable names to (1) be valid variable names and follow (2) conventions of writing variable names.

✓ 23doctor

✓ line1

✓ Option3

✓ Mydesk

✓ #cup3

Practice Exercise 2

Write/Suggest variable names that are (1) valid and (2) conventional.

✓ You want to sum three numbers.

✓ You want to store the names of four students.

✓ You want to store the names of five doctors in a hospital.

Keywords and Identifiers in Python Programming Language

At this point, you have been wondering why you must use print and str in that manner without the freedom or knowledge of why the stated words have to be written in that manner. The words print and str constitute a special type of words that have to be written that way always. Each programming language has its set of keywords. In most cases, some keywords are found across several programming languages. Keywords are case sensitive in python meaning that we have to type them in their lowercase form always. Keywords cannot be used to name a function (we will explain what it is later), name of a variable.

There are 33 keywords in Python and all are in lowercase save for None, False, and True. They must always be written as they appear below:

Note: The print() and str are functions, but they are inbuilt/preloaded functions in Pythons. Functions are a set of rules and methods that act when invoked. For instance, the print function will display output when activated/invoked/called. At this point, you have not encountered all of the keywords, but you will meet them gradually. Take time to skim through, read and try to recall as many as you can.

Practice Exercise

Identify what is wrong with the following variable names (The exercise requires recalling what we have learned so far)

- ✓ for=1
- ✓ yield=3
- ✓ 34ball
- ✓ m

Comments and Statements

Statements in Python

A statement in Python refers to instructions that a Python interpreter can work on/execute. An example is str='I am a Programmer' and number1=3. A statement having an equal sign(=) is known as an assignment statement. They are other types of statements such as the if, while, and for which will be handled later.

Practice Exercise

- ✓ Write a Python statement that assigns the first number a value of 18.

- ✓ Write a programming statement that assigns the second number value of 21.
- ✓ What type of statements are a. and b. above?

Multi-Line Python Statement

It is possible to spread a statement over multiple lines. Such a statement is known as a multi-line statement. The termination of a programming statement is denoted by new line character. To spread a statement overs several lines, in Python, we use the backslash (\) known as the line continuation character. An example of a multi-line statement is:

sum=3+6+7+\

9+1+3+\

11+4+8

The example above is also known as an explicit line continuation. In Python, the square brackets [] denotes line continuation similar to parenthesis/round brackets (), and lastly braces {}. The above example can be rewritten as

sum=(3+6+7+

9+1+3+

11+4+8)

Note: We have dropped the backslash(\) known as the line continuation character when we use the parenthesis(round brackets) because the parenthesis is doing the work that the line continuation \ was doing.

Question: Why do you think multi-line statements are necessary we can simply write a single line and the program statement will run just fine?

Answer: Multi-line statements can help improve formatting/readability of the entire program. Remember, when writing a program always assume that it is other people who will use and maintain it without your input.

Practice Exercise:

Rewrite the following program statements using multi-line operators such as the \, [],() or {} to improve readability of the program statements.

- total=2+9+3+6+8+2+5+1+14+5+21+26+4+7+13+31+24
- count=13+1+56+3+7+9+5+12+54+4+7+45+71+4+8+5

Semicolons are also used when creating multiple statements in a single line. Assume we have to assign and display the age of four employees in a python program. The program could be written as:

employee1=25; employee2=45; employee3=32; employee4=43.

Indentation in Python

Indentation is used for categorization program lines into a block in Python. The amount of indentation to use in Python depends entirely on the programmer. However, it is important to ensure consistency. By convention, four whitespaces are used for indentation instead of using tabs. For example:

Note: We will explain what kind of program of this is later.

Indentation in Python also helps make the program look neat and clean. Indentation creates consistency. However, when performing line continuation indentation can be ignored. Incorrect indentation will create an indentation error. Correct python programs without indentation will still run but they might be neat and consistent from human readability view.

Comments in Pythons

When writing python programs and indeed any programming language, comments are very important. Comments are used to describe what is happening within a program. It becomes easier for another person taking a look at a program to have an idea of what the program does by reading the comments in it. Comments are also useful to a programmer as one can forget the critical details of a program written. The hash (#) symbol is used before writing a comment in Python. The comment extends up to the newline character. The python interpreter normally ignores comments. Comments are meant for programmers to understand the program better.

Example

I.   Start IDLE

II.   Navigate to the File menu and click New Window

III.   Type the following:

#This is my first comment

#The program will print Hello World

Print('Hello World')   #This is an inbuilt function to display

IV.   On the file, menu click Save. Type the name of myProgram5.py

Navigate to Run and click Run Module to run the program

Practice Exercise

This exercise integrates most of what we have covered so far.

- ✓ Write a program to sum two numbers 45, and 12 and include single line comments at each line of code.
- ✓ Write a program to show the names of two employees where the first employee is "Daisy" and the second employee is "Richard". Include single comments at each line of code.
- ✓ Write a program to display the student registration numbers where the student names and their registration are: Yvonne=235, Ian=782, James=1235, Juliet=568.

Multi-Line Comments

Just like multi-line program statements we also have multi-line comments. There are several ways of writing multi-line comments. The first approach is to type the hash (#) at each comment line starting point.

For Example

Start IDLE.

Navigate to the File menu and click New Window.

Type the following:

#I am going to write a long comment line

#the comment will spill over to this line

#and finally end here.

The second way of writing multi-line comments involves using triple single or double quotes: '" or"'"'. For multi-line strings and multi-line comments in Python, we use the triple quotes. Caution: When used in docstrings they will generate extra code but we do not have to worry about this at this instance.

Example:

Start IDLE.

Navigate to the File menu and click New Window.

Type the following:

""""This is also a great i

illustration of

a multi-line comment in Python""""

Summary

Variable are storage locations that a user specifies before writing and running a python program. Variable names are labels of those storage locations. A variable holds a value depending on circumstances. For instance, doctor1 can be Daniel, Brenda or Rita. Patient1 can be Luke, William or Kelly. Variable names are written by adhering to rules and conventions. Rules are a must while conventions are optional but recommended as they help write readable variable names. When writing a program, you should assume that another person will examine or run it without your input and thus should be well written. The next chapter will discuss Variables. In programming, declaring variables means that we explicitly state the nature of the variable. The variable can be declared as an integer, long integer, short integer, floating integer, a string, or as a character including if it is accessible locally or globally. A variable is a storage location that changes values depending on conditions. Use descriptive names when writing your variables.

SECOND DAY

Part 4: Data Types in Python

Numbers

As indicated, Python accommodates floating, integer and complex numbers. The presence or absence of a decimal point separates integers and floating points. For instance, 4 is integer while 4.0 is a floating point number.

On the other hand, complex numbers in Python are denoted as r+tj where j represents the real part and t is the virtual part. In this context the function type() is used to determine the variable class. The Python function instance() is invoked to make a determination of which specific class function originates from.

Example:

Start IDLE.

Navigate to the File menu and click New Window.

Type the following:

number=6

  print(type(number))   #should output class int

print(type(6.0))   #should output class float

complex_num=7+5j

print(complex_num+5)

print(isinstance(complex_num, complex)) #should output True

Important: Integers in Python can be of infinite length. Floating numbers in Python are assumed precise up to fifteen decimal places.

Number Conversion

This segment assumes you have prior basic knowledge of how to manually or using a calculate to convert decimal into binary, octal and hexadecimal. Check out the Windows Calculator in Windows 10, Calculator version Version 10.1804.911.1000 and choose programmer mode to automatically convert.

Programmers often need to convert decimal numbers into octal, hexadecimal and binary forms. A prefix in Python allows denotation of these numbers to their corresponding type.

Number System Prefix

Octal   '0O' or '0o'

Binary   '0B' or '0b'

Hexadecimal   '0X or '0x'

Example

print(0b1010101) #Output:85

print(0x7B+0b0101) #Output: 128 (123+5)

print(0o710) #Output:710

Practice Exercise

Write a Python program to display the following:

- 0011 11112
- 747
- 9316

Type Conversion

Sometimes referred to as coercion, type conversion allows us to change one type of number into another. The preloaded functions such as float(), int() and complex() enable implicit and explicit type conversions. The same functions can be used to change from strings.

Example:

Start IDLE.

Navigate to the File menu and click New Window.

Type the following:

int(5.3)   #Gives 5

int(5.9)   #Gives 5

The int() will produce a truncation effect when applied to floating numbers. It will simply drop the decimal point part without rounding off. For the float() let us take a look:

Start IDLE.

Navigate to the File menu and click New Window.

Type the following:

float(6)   #Gives 6.0

ccomplex('4+2j') #Gives (4+2j)

Practice Exercise

Apply the int() conversion to the following:

- ✓ 4.1
- ✓ 4.7
- ✓ 13.3
- ✓ 13.9

Apply the float() conversion to the following:

- ✓ 7
- ✓ 16
- ✓ 19

Decimal in Python

Example

Start IDLE.

Navigate to the File menu and click New Window.

Type the following:

(1.2+2.1)==3.3 #Will return False, why?

Discussion

The computer works with finite numbers and fractions cannot be stored in their raw form as they will create infinite long binary sequence.

Fractions in Python

The fractions module in Python allows operations on fractional numbers.

Example

Start IDLE.

Navigate to the File menu and click New Window.

Type the following:

import fractions

print(fractions.my_fraction(2.5))   #Output 5/2

print(fractions.my_fraction(4))   #Output 5

print(fractions.my_fraction(2,5))   #output 2/5

NOTE
Creating my_fraction from float can lead to unusual results due to the misleading representation of binary floating point.

Mathematics in Python

To carry out mathematical functions, Python offers modules like random and math.

Start IDLE.

Navigate to the File menu and click New Window.

Type the following:

import math

print(math.pi)   #output:3.14159....

print(math.cos(math.pi)) #the output will be -1.0

print(math.exp(10)) #the output will be 22026.4....

print(math.log10(100)) #the output will be 2

print(math.factorial(5)) #the output will be 120

Practice Exercise

Write a python program that uses math functions from the math module to perform the following:

- ✓ Square of 34
- ✓ Log1010000
- ✓ Cos 45 x sin 90
- ✓ Exponent of 20

Before tackling flow control, it is important we explore logical operators.

Comparison operators are special operators in Python programming language that evaluate to either True or False state of the condition.

Program flow control refers to a way in which a programmer explicitly species the order of execution of program code lines. Normally, flow control involves placing some condition (s) on the program code lines. In this chapter, we will explore and test various flow controls in Python.

Summary

In this tutorial, you learned about the built-in **data types** and **functions** Python provides.

The examples given so far have all manipulated and displayed only constant values. In most programs, you are usually going to want to create objects that change in value as the program executes.

Part 5: Loops and Functions

LOOPS

if...else Flow Control

The if..else statement in Python is a decision making when executing the program. The if...else statement will ONLY execute code if the specified condition exists.

The syntax of if...else in Python

if test expression:

Statement(s)

Discussion

The python program will only execute the statements(s) if the test expression is True. The program first evaluates the test expression before executing the statement(s). The program will not execute the statement(s) if the test expression is False. By convention, the body of it is marked by indentation while the first is not indented line signals the end.

Challenge: Think of scenarios, real-life, where the if...else condition is required.

• If you have not enrolled for a course, then you cannot sit for the exam else sit for the exam.

• If you have paid for house rent then you will be issued with acknowledgment receipt else request for more time.

• If you are a licensed driver then you can drive to school else you hire a taxi.

• If you are tired then you can watch movies else can complete the essay.

• If you are an ethical person then you will acknowledge your mistake else you will overlook the damage caused.

- If you are committed to programming then you will practice daily else you will lose interest.

- If you have signed for email alerts you will be updated frequently else you will have to check the website daily.

- If you plead guilty to all accounts you are likely to be convicted else the merit of your case will depend on cross-examination of witnesses and evidence presented.

Note: When we use the if statement alone without the else part, it will only print/display if the condition is true, it will not cater for the alternative, the case where the first condition is not present.

Example 1

Start IDLE.

Navigate to the File menu and click New Window.

Type the following:

number=5

if number>0   #The comparison operator

   print(number, "The number is a positive number")

Discussion

The program contains the if the condition that tests if the given number satisfies the if condition, "is it greater than 0" since 5 is greater than zero, the condition is satisfied the interpreter is allowed to execute the next statement which is to extract and display the numerical value including the string message. The test condition in this program is "number>0. But think of when the condition is not met, what happens? Let us look at Example 2.

Example 2

Start IDLE.

Navigate to the File menu and click New Window.

Type the following:

number=-9

if number>0:

  print(number, "This is a positive number")

Discussion

The program contains only the if statement which tests the expression by testing of -9 is greater than zero since it is not the interpreter will not execute the subsequent program code lines. In real life, you will want to provide for an alternate in case the first condition is not met. This program will not display anything when executed because the if the condition has not been met. The test condition in this program is "number>0.

Practice Exercise

Write programs in Python using if statement only to perform the following:

- Given number=7, write a program to test and display only even numbers.
- Given number1=8, number2=13, write a program to only display if the sum is less than 10.
- Given count_int=57, write a program that tests if the count is more than 45 and displays, the count is above the recommended number.
- Given marks=34, write a program that tests if the marks are less than 50 and display the message, the score is below average.
- Given marks=78, write a program that tests if the marks are more than 50 and display the message, great performance.

- Given number=88, write a program that tests if the number is an odd number and displays the message, Yes it is an odd number.

- Given number=24, write a program that tests and displays if the number is even.

- Given number =21, write a program that tests if the number is odd and displays the string, Yes it is an odd number.

Note

The execution of statements after the if expression will only happen where the if the expression evaluates to True, otherwise the statements are ignored.

if...else Statement in Python

The if...else syntax

if test condition:

  Statements

else:

  Statements

The explanation the if statement, the if...else statement will execute the body of if in the case that the tests condition is True. Should the if...else tests expression evaluate to false, the body of the else will be executed. Program blocks are denoted by indentation. The if...else provides more maneuverability when placing conditions on the code.

Example

A program that checks whether a number is positive or negative

Start IDLE.

Navigate to the File menu and click New Window.

Type the following:

number_mine=-56

if(number<0):

  print(number_mine, "The number is negative")

else:

  print(number_mine, "The number is a positive number")

Practice Exercise

Write a Python program that uses if..else flow control to perform the following

- ✓ Given number=9, write a program that tests and displays whether the number is even or odd.
- ✓ Given marks=76, write a program that tests and displays whether the marks are above pass mark or not bearing in mind that pass mark is 50.
- ✓ Given number=78, write a program that tests and displays whether the number is even or odd.
- ✓ Given marks=27, write a program that tests and displays whether the marks are above pass mark or not bearing in mind that pass mark is 50.

Challenge:

Write a program that accepts age input from the user, explicitly coverts the age into integer data types, then uses if...else flow control to tests whether the person is underage or not, the legal age is 21. Include comments and indentation to improve the readability of the program.

if...elif...else Flow Control Statement in Python

Now think of scenarios where we need to evaluate multiple conditions, not just one, not just two but three and more. Think of where you have to choose team member, if not Richard, then Mercy, if not Richard and Mercy then Brian, if not Richard, Mercy, and Brian then Yvonne. Real-life scenarios may involve several choices/conditions that have to be captured when writing a program.

if...elif..else Syntax

if test expression:

    Body of if

elif test expression:

    Body of elif

else:

    Body of else

Remember that the elif simply refers to else if and is intended to allow for checking of multiple expressions. The if the block is evaluated first, then elif block(s), before the else block. In this case, the else block is more of a fallback option when all other conditions return false. Important to remember, despite several blocks available in if..elif..else only one block will be executed.

Example:

Three conditions covered but the only one can execute at a given instance.

Start IDLE.

Navigate to the File menu and click New Window.

Type the following:

number_mine=87

if(number>0):

  print(number_mine, "This is a positive number")

elif(number_mie==0):

  print(number_mine, "The number is zero")

else:

  print(number_mine, "The number is a negative number")

Discussion:

There are three possibilities but at any given instance the only condition will exist and this qualifies the use of if family flow control statement. For three or more conditions to evaluate, the if...elif..else flow statement merits.

Nested if Statements in Python

Sometimes it happens that a condition exists but there are more sub-conditions that need to be covered and this leads to a concept known as nesting. The amount of statements to nests is not limited but you should exercise caution as you will realize nesting can lead to user errors when writing code. Nesting can also complicate maintaining of code. The only indentation can help determine the level of nesting.

Example

Start IDLE.

Navigate to the File menu and click New Window.

Type the following:

my_charact=str(input("Type a character here either 'a', 'b' or 'c':"))

if (my_charact='a'):

  if(my_charact='a'):

```
    print("a")

  else if:

    (my_charact='b')

    print("b")

else:

  print("c")
```

Practice Exercise

Write a program that uses the if..else flow control statement to check non-leap year and display either scenario. Include comments and indentation to enhance the readability of the program.

For Loop in Python

Indentation is used to separate the body of for loop in Python.

Note: Simple linear list takes the following syntax:

Variable_name=[values separated by a comma]

Example

Start IDLE.

Navigate to the File menu and click New Window.

Type the following:

numbers=[12, 3,18,10,7,2,3,6,1]   #Variable name storing the list

sum=0   #Initialize sum before usage, very important

for cumulative in numbers: #Iterate over the list

sum=sum+cumulative

print("The sum is" ,sum)

Practice Exercise

Start IDLE.

Navigate to the File menu and click New Window.

Type the following:

Write a Python program that uses the for loop to sum the following lists.

- ✓ marks=[3, 8,19, 6,18,29,15]
- ✓ ages=[12,17,14,18,11,10,16]
- ✓ mileage=[15,67,89,123,76,83]
- ✓ cups=[7,10,3,5,8,16,13]

range() function in Python

The range function (range()) in Python can help generate numbers. Remember in programming the first item is indexed 0. Therefore, range(11) will generate numbers from 0 to 10.

Example

Start IDLE.

Navigate to the File menu and click New Window.

Type the following:

print(range(7))

The output will be 0,1,2,3,4,5,6

Practice Exercise:

Without writing and running a Python program what will be the output for:

- ✓ range(16)
- ✓ range(8)
- ✓ range(4)

Using range() and len() and indexing

Practice Exercise

Write a Python program to iterate through the following list and include the message I listen to (each of the music genre). Use the for loop, len() and range(). Refer to the previous example on syntax.

folders=['Rumba', 'House', 'Rock']

Using for Loop with Else

It is possible to include a for loop with else but as an option. The else block will be executed if the items contained in the sequence are exhausted.

Example

Start IDLE.

Navigate to the File menu and click New Window.

Type the following:

marks=[12, 15,17]

for i in marks:

  print(i)

else:

   print("No items left")

Challenge:

Write a Python program that prints all prime numbers between 1 and 50.

While Loop in Python

In Python, the while loop is used to iterate over a block of program code as long as the test condition stays True. The while loop is used in contexts where the user does not know the loop cycles required. As earlier indicated, the while loop body is determined through indentation.

Example

Start IDLE.

Navigate to the File menu and click New Window.

Type the following:

Caution: Failing to include the value of the counter will lead to an infinite loop.

Practice Exercise

- Write a Python program that utilizes the while flow control statement to display the sum of all odd numbers from 1 to 10.

- Write a Python program that employs the while flow control statement to display the sum of all numbers from 11 to 21.

- Write a Python program that incorporates while flow control statement to display the sum of all even numbers from 1 to 10.

Using While Loop with Else

If the condition is false and no break occurs, a while loop's else part runs.

Example

Start IDLE.

Navigate to the File menu and click New Window.

Type the following:

track = 0

```
while track< 4:

  print("Within the loop")

track = track + 1

else:

  print("Now within the else segment")
```

Python's Break and Continue

Let us use real-life analogy where we have to force a stop on iteration before it evaluates completely. Think of when cracking/breaking passwords using a simple dictionary attack that loops through all possible character combinations, you will want the program immediately it strikes the password searched without having to complete. Again, think of when recovering photos you accidentally deleted using a recovery software, you will want the recovery to stop iterating through files immediately it finds items within the specified range. The break and continue statement in Python works in a similar fashion.

Example

Start IDLE.

Navigate to the File menu and click New Window.

Type the following:

for tracker in "bring":

if tracker == "i":

break

print(tracker)

print("The End")

Continue Statement in Python

When the continue statement is used, the interpreter skips the rest of the code inside a loop for the current iteration only and the loop does not terminate. The loop continues with next iteration.

The syntax of Python continue

continue

Example

Start IDLE.

Navigate to the File menu and click New Window.

Type the following:

for tracker in "bring":

   if tracker == "i":

      continue

   print(tracker)

print("Finished")

The output of this program will be:

b

r

n

g

Finished

Analogy: Assume that you are running data recovery software and have specified skip word files (.doc, dox extension). The program will have to continue iterating even after skipping word files.

Practice Exercise

- Write a Python program using for loop that will break after striking "v" in the string "Oliver".
- Write a Python program that will continue after skipping "m" in the string "Lemon".

Pass Statement in Python

Like a comment, a pass statement does not impact the program as it leads to no operation.

The syntax of pass

pass

Think of a program code that you plan to use in future but is not currently needed. Instead of having to insert that code in future, the code can be written as pass statements.

Example

Start IDLE.

Navigate to the File menu and click New Window.

Type the following:

my_list={'k','i','n'}

for tracker in my_list:

  pass

Functions in Python

Functions in Python help split large code into smaller units. Functions make a program more organized and easy to manage.

In Python functions will assume the syntax form below:

def name_of_function (arguments):

  """docstring"""

statements(s)

Example

Start IDLE.

Navigate to the File menu and click New Window.

Type the following:

```python
def welcome(salute):

    """The Python function welcomes you to

    the individual passed in as

    parameter"""

    print("Welcome " + salute + ". Lovely Day!")
```

Calling a Function in Python

We can call a function once we have defined it from another function or program.

Calling a function simply involves typing the function name with suitable parameters.

Start IDLE.

Navigate to the File menu and click New Window.

Type the following:

welcome('Brenda')

The output will be "Welcome Brenda. Lovely Day!'

Practice Exercise

Write a function that when called outputs"Hello (student name), kindly submit your work by Sunday".

Docstring

It is placed after the function header as the first statement and explains in summary what the function does. Docstring should always be placed between triple quotes to accommodate multiple line strings.

Calling/Invoking the docstring we typed earlier

Example

Start IDLE.

Navigate to the File menu and click New Window.

Type the following:

print(welcome._doc_)

The output will be "This function welcomes you to

the individual passed in as

parameter".

The syntax for calling/invoking the docstring is:

print(function_name. _doc_)

Python Function Return Statement

Return syntax

return [list of expressions]

Discussion

The return statement can return a value or a None object.

Example

Print(welcome("Richard"))   #Passing arguments and calling the function

Welcome Richard. Lovely Day!

None   #the returned value

Random Function in Python

Start IDLE.

Navigate to the File menu and click New Window.

Type the following:

import math

print(random.shuffle_num(11, 21))

y=['f','g','h','m']

print(random.pick(y))

random.anypic(y)

print(y)

print(your_pick.random())

Iterators

In Python, iterator refers to objects that can be iterated upon.

The for loop is used to implement iterators in Python anywhere. Iterators in Python can also be implemented using generators and comprehensions. In Python, an iterator concerns an construct that can be called several times performing same action.

Iterators in Python implement the _iter_() special method and _next_() special method which is collectively referred to as the iterator protocol.

In Python, an object becomes iterable if we can get an iterator from it for example string, tuple, and list is iterable. In operation, the iter() function calls the _iter_() method and returns an iterator from the set or list or string.

Manually Iterating Through Items in Python

The next() function is used in Python to manually loop through all the items of an iterator

Example

list_mine = [14, 17, 10, 13]

iter_list = iter(list_mine)

print(next(iter_list))

print(next(iter_list))

print(my_iter.__next__())

print(my_iter.__next__())

next(iter_list)

NOTE

The for loop provides an efficienty ay of automatically iterating through a list. The for loop can be applied on a file, list or string among others in Python.

Example

for element in list_mine:

    print(element)

Explaining the Loop

The for loop gets to iterate automatically through the Python list.

Example

for element in list_mine:

object_iter = iter(iterable)

while True:

    try:

element = next(object_iter)

except StopIteration:

break

Creating Custom Iterator in Python

On the other hand, the _next_() will scan and give the next element in the sequence and will trigger the StopIteration exception once it reaches the end.

Example

class Power:

   """Will implement powers of 2

   """

   def __init__(self, max = 0):

     self.max = max

   def __iter__(self):

     self.m = 0

     return self

```
def __next__(self):

    if self.m <= self.max:

        result = 2 ** self.m

        self.m += 1

        return result

    else:

        raise StopIteration
```

Discussion

Example

```
for j in Power(5):

    print(j)
```

Infinite Iterators

There may be situations that require continuous iteration. The situations we have tackled so far were infinite iterators and had to terminate after exhausting the items in the iterable. The iter() is an inbuilt function. The method is fired by providing two arguments. The first argument in iter() is the one being called while the other argument acts as a sentinel. Until the function returns a value equal to the Sentinel, the iterator will continue calling the function.

Example

int()

infer = iterate(int,2)

next(infer)

next(infer)

Discussion

The int() function in this program will always return value 0. Therefore, passing the function as iterate(int, 2) will return an iterator that invokes int(). The calling of int() will stop when the returned value equals 2. Since this will never happen, we will end up with an infinite iterator.

Example

Assume we want to display all odd numbers that exist.

Practice Exercise

Write a Python program that uses a custom infinite iterator to display all even numbers.

Closure Function in Python

Example

def printing(msg):

def printers():

print(msg)

return printer

custom = printing("Welcome")

custom()

Discussion

The printing() function was invoked with the string "Welcome" that gives us objects associated with the name. Calling custom() implied the message was remembered even though it had already completed executing the printing()

function. In Python, the technique via which part of the data gets tied to the code is termed as closure. In this case, even when the variable gets out of scope, the value in the enclosing scope is remembered.

Example

del printing

another()

printing("Welcome")

NOTE

In Python, closures help provide a limited form of encapsulation. The use of enclosures can help avoid wide usage of global scope variables. Remember global scope implies that the names are accessible and modifiable at any part of the program which can create inconsistency. Closures can also be used to give an object-oriented solution to a problem.

Example

def product(n):

  def times(y):

    return y number*

```
    return times

multiply1 = times(13)

multiply1 = times(15)

print(multiply2(19))

print(multiply2(13))

print(multiply2(multiply(12)))
```

Projects

1. Implementing   Simple   Calculator   in   Python

```
def sum(m, n):

    return m + n

def minus(m, n):

    return m - n

def product(m, n):

    return m * n
```

```python
def division(m, n):

    return m / n

print("Choose an Operation.")

print("1.Sum")

print("2.Minus")

print("3.Product")

print("4.Division")

option = input("Type your choice (1/2/3/4):")

number1 = int(input("Enter number 1: "))

number2 = int(input("Enter number 2: "))

if option == '1':

    print(number1,"+",number2,"=", sum(number1,number2))

elif option == '2':

    print(number1,"-",number2,"=", minus(num1,num2))

elif choice == '3':
```

```
                    print(number1,"*",number2,"=",
product(number1,number2))

elif choice == '4':

                    print(number1,"/",number2,"=",
division(number1,number2))

else:

    print("Check Your Selection, Out of Range")
```

2. Program to return factors of any integer

```
def factors(m):

    print("We found factors of",m,"as:")

    for j in range(1, m + 1):

        if m % j == 0:

            print(j)

number = 400

factors(number)
```

Summary

For loops can iterate over a sequence of numbers using the "range" and "xrange" functions. The difference between range and xrange is that the range function returns a new list with numbers of that specified range, whereas xrange returns an iterator, which is more efficient. (Python 3 uses the range function, which acts like xrange). Note that the range function is zero based.

THIRD DAY

Part 6: Variable Scope and Lifetime in Python Functions

Variables and parameters defined within a Python function have local scope implying they are not visible from outside. In Python the variable lifetime is valid as long the function executes and is the period throughout that a variable exists in memory. Returning the function destroys the function variables.

Example

Start IDLE.

Navigate to the File menu and click New Window.

Type the following:

```
def function_my()

    marks=15

print("The value inside the function is:", marks)

marks=37

function_my()

print"The value outside the function is:",marks)
```

Function Types

They are broadly grouped into user-defined and built-in functions. The built-in functions are part of the Python interpreter while the user-defined functions are specified by the user.

Practice Exercise

Give three examples of built-in functions in Pythons

Function Argument

Calling a function requires passing the correct number of parameters otherwise the interpreter will generate an error.

Ilustration

Start IDLE.

Navigate to the File menu and click New Window.

Type the following:

def salute(name,mesage):

  """This function welcomes to

  the student with the provided message"""

  print("Welcome",salute + ', ' + message)

welcome("Brenda","Lovely Day!")

Note: The function welcome() has two parameters. We will not get any error as has been fed with two arguments. Let us try calling the function with one argument and see what happens:

welcome("Brenda")   #only one argument passed

Running this program will generate an error saying "TypeError: welcome() missing 1 required positional argument. The same will happen when we pass no arguments to the function.

Example 2

Start IDLE.

Navigate to the File menu and click New Window.

Type the following:

welcome()

The interpreter will generate an error "TypeError: welcome() missing 2 required positional arguments".

Keywords Arguments in Python

Python provides a way of calling functions using keyword arguments. When calling functions using keyword arguments, the order of arguments can be changed. The values of a function are matched to the argument position-wise.

Note:

In the previous example function welcome when invoked as welcome("Brenda", "Lovely Day!"). The value "Brenda" is assigned to the argument name and "Lovely Day!" to msg.

Calling the function using keywords

Start IDLE.

Navigate to the File menu and click New Window.

Type the following:

welcome(name="Brenda", msg="Lovely Day!")

Keywords not following the order

welcome(msg="Lovely Day!", name="Brenda")

Arbitrary Arguments

It may happen that we do not have knowledge of all arguments needed to be passed into a function. Analogy: Assume that you are writing a program to welcome all new students this semester. In this case, you do not how many will report.

Example

Start IDLE.

Navigate to the File menu and click New Window.

Type the following:

def welcome(*names):

""""This welcome function salutes all students in the names tuple.""""

  for name in names:

    print("Welcome".name)

welcome("Lucy","Richard","Fridah","James")

The output of the program will be:

Welcome Lucy

Welcome Richard

Welcome Fridah

Welcome James

Recursion in Python

The definition of something in terms of itself is called recursion. A recursive function calls other functions.

Example

Python program to compute integer factorials

Practice Exercise

Write a Python program to find the factorial of 7.

Python Anonymous Function

Some functions may be specified devoid of a name and this are called anonymous function. The lambda keyword is used to denote an anonymous function. Anonymous functions are also referred to as lambda functions in Python.

Syntax

lambda arguments: expression.

Lambda functions must always have one expression but can have several arguments.

Example

Start IDLE.

Navigate to the File menu and click New Window.

85

Type the following:

*double = lambda y: y * 2*

 # Output: 10

print(double(5))

Example 2

We can use inbuilt functions such as filter () and lambda to show only even numbers in a list/tuple.

Start IDLE.

Navigate to the File menu and click New Window.

Type the following:

first_marks = [3, 7, 14, 16, 18, 21, 13, 32]

fresh_marks = list(filter(lambda n: (n%2 == 0) , first_marks))

 # Output: [14, 16, 18, 32]

print(fresh_marks)

Lambda function and map() can be used to double individual list items.

Example 3

Start IDLE.

Navigate to the File menu and click New Window.

Type the following:

first_score = [3, 7, 14, 16, 18, 21, 13, 32]

fresh_score = list(map(lambda m: m * 2 , first_score))

 # Output: [6, 14, 28, 32, 36, 42, 26, 64]

print(fresh_score)

Python's Global, Local, and Nonlocal

Python's Global Variables

Variables declared outside of a function in Python are known as global variables. They are declared in global scope. A global variable can be accessed outside or inside of the function.

Example

Start IDLE.

Navigate to the File menu and click New Window.

Type the following:

```
y= "global"

def foo():

    print("y inside the function :", y)

foo()

print("y outside the function:", y)
```

Discussion

In the illustration above, y is a global variable and is defined a foo() to print the global variable y. When we call the foo() it will print the value of y.

Local Variables

A local variable is declared within the body of the function or in the local scope.

Example

Start IDLE.

Navigate to the File menu and click New Window.

Type the following:

def foo():

  x = "local"

foo()

print(x)

Discussion

Running this program will generate an error indicating 'x' is undefined. The error is occurring because we are trying to access local variable x in a global scope whereas foo() functions only in the local scope.

Creating a Local Variable in Python

Example

A local variable is created by declaring a variable within the function.

def foo():

Start IDLE.

Navigate to the File menu and click New Window.

Type the following:

```
x = "local"

print(x)
foo()
```

Discussion

When we execute the code, the output will be:

Local

Python's Global and Local Variable

Using both local and global variables in the same code.

Example

Start IDLE.

Navigate to the File menu and click New Window.

Type the following:

```
y = "global"

def foo():

    global y

    x = "local"

    y = y * 2

    print(y)

    print(x)

foo()
```

Discussion

The output of the program will be:

global global

local

We declared y as a global variable and x as a local variable in the foo(). The * operator issued to modify the global variable y and finally, we printed both y and x.

Local and Global Variables with the same name

Start IDLE.

Navigate to the File menu and click New Window.

Type the following:

```
y=6

def foo():

y=11

  print("Local variable y-", y)

foo()

print("Global variable y-", y)
```

Python's Nonlocal Variables

A Python's nonlocal variable is used in a nested function whose local scope is unspecified. It is neither global nor local scope.

Example

Creating a nonlocal variable.

Start IDLE.

Navigate to the File menu and click New Window.

Type the following:

def outer():

   y = "local variable"

   def inner():

      nonlocal y

      y = "nonlocal variable"

      print("inner:", y)

   inner()

   print("outer scope:", y)

outer()

Global Keyword in Python

The global keyword I Python allows modification of the variable outside the current scope. The global keyword makes changes to the variable in a local context. There are rules when creating a global keyword:

A global keyword is local by default when we create a variable within a function.

It is global by default when we define a variable outside of a function and you do not need to use the global keyword.

The global keyword is used to read and write a global variable within a function.

The use of global keyword outside a function will have no effect.

Example

Start IDLE.

Navigate to the File menu and click New Window.

Type the following:

number = 3   #A global variable

def add():

  print(number)

add()

The output of this program will be 3.

Modifying global variable from inside the function.

```
number=3              #a global variable

def add():

  number= number + 4    # add 4 to 3

  print(number)

add()
```

Discussion

When the program is executed it will generate an error indicating that the local variable number is referenced before assignment. The reason for encountering the error is because we can only access the global variable but are unable to modify it from inside the function. Using a global keyword would solve this.

Example

Start IDLE.

Navigate to the File menu and click New Window.

Type the following:

Modifying global variable within a function using the global keyword

```
number = 3          # a global variable

def add():

    global number

    number = number + 1 # increment by 1

    print("Inside the function add():", number)

add()

print("In main area:", number)
```

Discussion

When the program is run, the output will be:

Inside the function add(): 4

In the main area: 4

We defined a number as a global keyword within the function add(). The variable was then incremented by 1, variable number. Then we called the add () function to print global variable c.

Creating Global Variables across Python Modules

We can create a single module config.py that will contain all global variables and share the information across several modules within the same program.

Example

Start IDLE.

Navigate to the File menu and click New Window.

Type the following:

Create config.py

x=0

y="empty"

Then create an update.py file to modify global variables

Import config

config.x=11

config.y="Today"

Then create a main.py file to evaluate the changes in value

import config

import update

print(config.x)

print(config.y)

Discussion

Running the main.py file will generate:

11

Today

Python Modules

Modules consist of definitions as well as program statements.

An illustration is a file name config.py which is considered as a module. The module name would be config. Modules are sued to help break large programs into smaller manageable and organized files as well as promoting reusability of code.

Example:

Creating the First module

Start IDLE.

Navigate to the File menu and click New Window.

Type the following:

Def add(x, y):

"""This is a program to add two

  numbers and return the outcome"""

outcome=x+y

return outcome

Module Import

The keyword import is used to import.

Example

Import first

The dot operator can help us access a function as long as we know the name of the module.

Example

Start IDLE.

Navigate to the File menu and click New Window.

Type the following:

first.add(6,8)

Import Statement in Python

The import statement can be used to access the definitions within a module via the dot operator.

Start IDLE.

Navigate to the File menu and click New Window.

Type the following:

import math

print("The PI value is", math.pi)

Import with renaming

Example

Start IDLE.

Navigate to the File menu and click New Window.

Type the following:

import math as h

  print("The PI value is-",h.pi)

Discussion

In this case, h is our renamed math module with a view helping save typing time in some instances. When we rename the new name becomes valid and recognized one and not the original one.

From...import statement Python.

It is possible to import particular names from a module rather than importing the entire module.

Example

Start IDLE.

Navigate to the File menu and click New Window.

Type the following:

from math import pi

print("The PI value is-", pi)

Importing all names

Example

Start IDLE.

Navigate to the File menu and click New Window.

Type the following:

from math import*

print("The PI value is-", pi)

Discussion

In this context, we are importing all definitions from a particular module but it is encouraged norm as it can lead to unseen duplicates.

Module Search Path in Python

Example

Start IDLE.

Navigate to the File menu and click New Window.

Type the following:

import sys

sys.path

Python searches everywhere including the sys file.

Reloading a Module

Python will only import a module once increasing efficiency in execution.

print("This program was executed")

import mine

Reloading Code

Example

Start IDLE.

Navigate to the File menu and click New Window.

Type the following:

import mine

import mine

import mine

mine.reload(mine)

Dir() built-in Python function

For discovering names contained in a module, we use the dir() inbuilt function.

Syntax

dir(module_name)

Python Package

Files in python hold modules and directories are stored in packages. A single package in Python holds similar modules. Therefore, different modules should be placed in different Python packages.

Summary

Parameters and **variables** defined inside a function is not visible from outside. Hence, they have a local **scope**. **Lifetime** of a **variable** is the period throughout which the **variable** exits in the memory. The **lifetime** of **variables** inside a function is as long as the function executes.

Part 7: Lists in Python

We create a list in Python by placing items called elements inside square brackets separated by commas. The items in a list can be of mixed data type.

Start IDLE.

Navigate to the File menu and click New Window.

Type the following:

list_mine=[]   #empty list

list_mine=[2,5,8] #list of integers

list_mine=[5,"Happy", 5.2] #list having mixed data types

Practice Exercise

Write a program that captures the following in a list: "Best", 26,89,3.9

Nested Lists

A nested list is a list as an item in another list.

Example

Start IDLE.

Navigate to the File menu and click New Window.

Type the following:

list_mine=["carrot", [9, 3, 6], ['g']]

Practice Exercise

Write a nested for the following elements:
[36,2,1],"Writer",'t',[3.0, 2.5]

Accessing Elements from a List

In programming and in Python specifically, the first time is always indexed zero. For a list of five items we will access them from index0 to index4. Failure to access the items in a list in this manner will create index error. The index is always an integer as using other number types will create a type error. For nested lists, they are accessed via nested indexing.

Example

Start IDLE.

Navigate to the File menu and click New Window.

Type the following:

list_mine=['b','e','s','t']

print(list_mine[0])   #the output will be b

print(list_mine[2])   #the output will be s

print(list_mine[3])   #the output will be t

Practice Exercise

Given the following list:

your_collection=['t','k','v','w','z','n','f']

- ✓ Write a Python program to display the second item in the list
- ✓ Write a Python program to display the sixth item in the last
- ✓ Write a Python program to display the last item in the list.

Nested List Indexing

Start IDLE.

Navigate to the File menu and click New Window.

Type the following:

```
nested_list=["Best",[4,7,2,9]]
```

```
print(nested_list[0][1]
```

Python Negative Indexing

For its sequences, Python allows negative indexing. The last item on the list is index-1, index -2 is the second last item and so on.

Start IDLE.

Navigate to the File menu and click New Window.

Type the following:

list_mine=['c','h','a','n','g','e','s']

print(list_mine[-1])   #Output is s

print(list_mine [-4]) ##Output is n

Slicing Lists in Python

Slicing operator(full colon) is used to access a range of elements in a list.

 Example

Start IDLE.

Navigate to the File menu and click New Window.

Type the following:

list_mine=['c','h','a','n','g','e','s']

print(list_mine[3:5])   #Picking elements from the 4 to the sixth

Example

Picking elements from start to the fifth

Start IDLE.

Navigate to the File menu and click New Window.

Type the following:

print(list_mine[:-6])

Example

Picking the third element to the last.

print(list_mine[2:])

Practice Exercise

Given class_names=['John', 'Kelly', 'Yvonne', 'Una','Lovy','Pius', 'Tracy']

- ✓ Write a python program using slice operator to display from the second students and the rest.
- ✓ Write a python program using slice operator to display first student to the third using negative indexing feature.
- ✓ Write a python program using slice operator to display the fourth and fifth students only.

Manipulating Elements in a List using the assignment operator

Items in a list can be changed meaning lists are mutable.

Start IDLE.

Navigate to the File menu and click New Window.

Type the following:

list_yours=[4,8,5,2,1]

list_yours[1]=6

print(list_yours)   #The output will be [4,6,5,2,1]

Changing a range of items in a list

Start IDLE.

Navigate to the File menu and click New Window.

Type the following:

list_yours[0:3]=[12,11,10] #Will change first item to fourth item in the list print(list_yours)   #Output will be: [12,11,10,1]

Appending/Extending items in the List

The append() method allows extending the items in the list. The extend() can also be used.

Example

Start IDLE.

Navigate to the File menu and click New Window.

Type the following:

list_yours=[4, 6, 5]

list_yours.append(3)

print(list_yours)   #The output will be [4,6,5, 3]

Example

Start IDLE.

Navigate to the File menu and click New Window.

Type the following:

list_yours=[4,6,5]

list_yours.extend([13,7,9])

print(list_yours)   #The output will be [4,6,5,13,7,9]

The plus operator(+) can also be used to combine two lists. The * operator can be used to iterate a list a given number of times.

Example

Start IDLE.

Navigate to the File menu and click New Window.

Type the following:

 list_yours=[4,6,5]

print(list_yours+[13,7,9]) # Output:[4, 6, 5,13,7,9]

*print(['happy']*4)   #Output:["happy","happy",*
"happy","happy"]

Removing or Deleting Items from a List

The keyword del is used to delete elements or the entire list in Python.

Example

Start IDLE.

Navigate to the File menu and click New Window.

Type the following:

list_mine=['t','r','o','g','r','a','m']

del list_mine[1]

print(list_mine) #t, o, g, r, a, m

Deleting Multiple Elements

Example

Start IDLE.

Navigate to the File menu and click New Window.

Type the following:

del list_mine[0:3]

Example

print(list_mine) #a, m

Delete Entire List

Start IDLE.

Navigate to the File menu and click New Window.

Type the following:

delete list_mine

print(list_mine) #will generate an error of lost not found

The remove() method or pop() method can be used to remove specified item. The pop() method will remove and return the last item if index is not given and helps implement lists as stacks. The clear() method is used to empty a list.

Start IDLE.

Navigate to the File menu and click New Window.

Type the following:

list_mine=['t','k','b','d','w','q','v']

list_mine.remove('t')

print(list_mine)   #output will be ['t','k','b','d','w','q','v']

print(list_mine.pop(1))   #output will be 'k'

print(list_mine.pop())   #output will be 'v'

Practice Exercise

Given list_yours=['K','N','O','C','K','E','D']

- ✓ Pop the third item in the list, save the program as list1.
- ✓ Remove the fourth item using remove() method and save the program as list2
- ✓ Delete the second item in the list and save the program as list3.
- ✓ Pop the list without specifying an index and save the program as list4.

Using Empty List to Delete an Entire or Specific Elements

Start IDLE.

Navigate to the File menu and click New Window.

Type the following:

list_mine=['t','k','b','d','w','q','v']

list_mine=[1:2]=[]

print(list_mine)   #Output will be ['t','w','q','v']

Practice Exercise

➢ Use list access methods to display the following items in reversed order list_yours=[4,9,2,1,6,7]

➢ Use list access method to count the elements in a.

➢ Use list access method to sort the items in a. in an ascending order/default.

Summary

Lists store an ordered collection of items which can be of different types. The list defined above has items that are all of the same type (int), but all the items of a list do not need to be of the same type as you can see below.

 # Define a list
heterogenousElements = [3, True, 'Michael', 2.0]

FOURTH DAY

Part 8: Tuples in Python

A tuple is like a list but we cannot change elements in a tuple.

Example

Start IDLE.

Navigate to the File menu and click New Window.

Type the following:

tuple_mine = (21, 12, 31)

print(tuple_mine)

tuple_mine = (31, "Green", 4.7)

print(tuple_mine)

Accessing Python Tuple Elements

Example

Start IDLE.

Navigate to the File menu and click New Window.

Type the following:

tuple_mine=['t','r','o','g','r','a','m']

    print(tuple_mine[1])   #output:'r'

    print(tuple_mine[3])   #output:'g'

Negative Indexing

Just like lists, tuples can also be indexed negatively.

Like lists, -1 refers to the last element on the list and -2 refer to the second last element.

Example

Start IDLE.

Navigate to the File menu and click New Window.

Type the following:

tuple_mine=['t','r','o','g','r','a','m']

print(tuple_mine [-2]) #the output will be 'a'

Slicing

The slicing operator, the full colon is used to access a range of items in a tuple.

Example

Start IDLE.

Navigate to the File menu and click New Window.

Type the following:

tuple_mine=['t','r','o','g','r','a','m']

print(tuple_mine [2:5]) #Output: 'o','g','r','a'

print(tuple_mine[:-4]) #'g','r','a','m'

NOTE

Tuple elements are immutable meaning they cannot be changed. However, we can combine elements in a tuple using +(concatenation operator). We can also repeat elements in a tuple using the * operator, just like lists.

Example

Start IDLE.

Navigate to the File menu and click New Window.

Type the following:

print((7, 45, 13) + (17, 25, 76))

*print(("Several",) * 4)*

NOTE

Since we cannot change elements in tuple, we cannot delete the elements too. However removing the full tuple can be attained using the kwyword del.

Example

Start IDLE.

Navigate to the File menu and click New Window.

Type the following:

t_mine=['t','k','q','v','y','c','d']

del t_mine

Available Tuple Methods in Python

They are only two methods available for working Python tuples.

count(y)

When called will give the item numbers that are equal to y.

index(y)

When called will give index first item index that is equal to y.

Example

Start IDLE.

Navigate to the File menu and click New Window.

Type the following:

t_mine=['t','k','q','v','y','c','d']

print(t_mine.count('t'))

print(t_mine.index('l'))

Testing Membership in Tuple

The keyword in us used to check the specified element exists in a tuple.

Start IDLE.

Navigate to the File menu and click New Window.

Type the following:

t_mine=['t','k','q','v','y','c','d']

print('a' t_mine) #Output: True

print('k' in t_mine) #Output: False

Inbuilt Python Functions with Tuple

String in Python.

Example

Start IDLE.

Navigate to the File menu and click New Window.

Type the following:

string_mine = 'Colorful'

print(string_mine)

string_mine = "Hello"

print(string_mine)

string_mine = "'Hello'"

print(string_mine)

string_mine = """I feel like I have

  been born a programmer"""

print(string_mine)

Accessing items in a string

Example

Start IDLE.

Navigate to the File menu and click New Window.

Type the following:

```
str = 'Colorful'

print('str = ', str)

print('str[1] = ', str[1])  #Output the second item

print('str[-2] = ', str[-2]) #Output the second last item

print('str[2:4] = ', str[2:4]) #Output the third through the fifth item
```

Deleting or Changing in Python

In Python, strings are immutable therefore cannot be changed once assigned. However, deleting the entire string is possible.

Example

Start IDLE.

Navigate to the File menu and click New Window.

Type the following:

del string_mine

The escape sequences enable us to format our output to enhance clarity to the human user. A program will still run successful without using escape sequences but the output will be highly confusing to the human user. Writing and displaying output in expected output is part of good programming practices. The following are commonly used escape sequences.

Examples

Start IDLE.

Navigate to the File menu and click New Window.

Type the following:

print("D:\\Lessons\\Programming")

print("Prints\n in two lines")

Summary

As earlier indicated earlier, integers, floating point, and complex numbers are supported in Python. There are integers, floating and complex classes that help convert different number data types. The presence or absence of a decimal point separates integers and floating points. For instance, 4 is integer while 4.0 is a floating point number. Programmers often need to convert decimal numbers into octal, hexadecimal and binary forms. We can represent binary, hexadecimal and octal systems in Python by simply placing a prefix to the particular number. Sometimes referred to as coercion, type conversion allows us to change one type of number into another.

Inbuilt functions such as int() allows us to convert data types directly. The same functions can be used to convert from strings. We create a list in Python by placing items called elements inside square brackets separated by commas. In programming and in Python specifically, the first time is always indexed zero. For a list of five items we will access them from index0 to index4. Failure to access the items in a list in this manner will create index error.

Part 9: Strings in Python

```python
def add5(x):
    return x+5

def dotwrite(ast):
    nodename = getNodename()
    label=symbol.sym_name.get(int(ast[0]),ast[0])
    print '    %s [label="%s' % (nodename, label),
    if isinstance(ast[1], str):
        if ast[1].strip():
            print '= %s"];' % ast[1]
        else:
            print '"]'
    else:
        print '"];'
        children = []
        for in n, childenumerate(ast[1:]):
            children.append(dotwrite(child))
        print ,'    %s -> {' % nodename
        for in :namechildren
            print '%s' % name,
```

A single or double quote in Python is used to indicate strings. The subsets of strings can be taken by using the slice operator ([:]) and []) with indexes beginning at () in the start of the string and operating their way from -1 at the end. Strings can be joined using the + (plus) sign known as the concatenation operator. The asterisk (*) is used as a repetition operator. Remember counting in programming starts from index zero (the first value)!

Example:

✓ Start IDLE

✓ Navigate to the File menu and click New Window

✓ Type the following:

```
str = 'Going Deep!'
print str              # Prints a complete string
print str[0]           # Prints first character of the string
print str[3:6]         # Prints characters starting from fourth to seventh
print str[3:]          # Prints string starting from the fourth character
print str * 3          # Prints string three times
print str + "I love Python" # Prints concatenated string
```

✓ On the file, menu click Save. Type the name of myProgram4.py

✓ Navigate to Run and click Run Module to run the program

The output of the program above should be:

Going Deep!

G

ng De

ng Deep!

Going Deep! Going Deep! Going Deep!

Going Deep! I love Python

Note: the # (hash sign) is used to indicate a single line comment. A comment is descriptive information about a particular line(s) of code. The comment is normally ignored by when running the program. The comment should be written after the # sign in python. Comments increase the readability of the program written.

Practice Exercise:

You will key in/type the following program statement:

str = 'I think I am now a Programmer'

a.   Write a program statement that will display the entire string/statement above.

b.   Write a program statement to display characters of the string from the second character to the sixth.

c.   Write a single program statement that will display the entire string two times. (use *).

d.   Write a program statement that will add the following at the end of the statement above, " of Python Programming Language"

String Operations

Several operations can be performed on a string making it a widely used datatype in Python.

Concatenation using the + operator, repetition using the * operator

Example

Start IDLE.

Navigate to the File menu and click New Window.

Type the following:

string1='Welcome'

string2='Again'

> *print('string1+string2=',string1+string2)*

*print(' string1 * 3 =', string1 * 3)*

Practice Exercise

Given string_a="I am awake" and string_b="coding in Python in a pajama"

String Iteration

The for control statement is used to continually scan through an entire scan until the specified number of times are reached before terminating the scan.

Membership Test in String

The keyword in is used to test if a sub string exists.

Example

't' in "triumph'   #Will return True

Inbuilt Python Functions for working with Strings

They include enumerate() and len().The len() function returns the length of the string.

String Formatting in Python

Single and Double Quotes

Example

Start IDLE.

Navigate to the File menu and click New Window.

Type the following:

print('They said, "We need a new team?"') # escape with single quotes

 # escaping double quotes

print("They said, \" We need a new team\"")

Python's Docstring

In Python, docstring refers to words offering a description and are written as the initial program statement in a function, module, method, or class definition. (We will handle this later on). Docstrings in Python are written using triple quotes.

Practice Exercise

This exercise will utilize several concepts that we covered earlier.

a.   Given the following program statement: Color1='red'; color1='blue'; CoLor1='yellow' explain why all the three will be treated as different variables in Python.

b. Consider the following Python program and identify what is wrong with it.

```python
student1_age=23          #This is the age of the first student

student2_age=19          #This is the age of the student

sotal_age=student1_age +student2_age    #Getting the sum of the ages of the

print(age)               #Displaying their ages
```

Part 10: Operators in Python

So far we have been using the summation (+) operator and it also doubles up as a concatenation operator (appending statements). However, we want to expand our list of operators and this leads us to basic operators in Python.

Arithmetic Operators

The multiplication (*), division (/), subtraction (-), and addition (+) are the arithmetic operators used to manipulate numbers.

Practice Exercise

Write the following programs and run it

- **Difference**

number1=35   #declaring first number

number2= 12   #declaring second number

difference=number2-number1   #declaring what the difference does

print(difference)   #Calling the print function to display what difference has

- **Multiplication**

number1=2   #declaring first number

number2= 15   #declaring second number

product=number1*number2   #declaring what the product does

print(product)   #Calling the print function to display what product has

- **Division**

number1=10   *#declaring first number*

number2= 50   *#declaring second number*

division=number2/number1   *#declaring what the division does*

print(division)   *#Calling the print function to display what product has*

Modulus

The modulus operator is used to return the integer remainder after division. The modulus=dividend%divisor.

Example

Start IDLE.

Navigate to the File menu and click New Window.

Type the following:

number1=2   *#declaring first number*

number2= 15   *#declaring second number*

remainder=number2%number1   *#declaring   what   the*
remainder does

print(remainder)   *#Calling the print function to display*
remainder has

Squaring and Cubing in Python

Squaring a number-number**2

Cubing a number-number**3

Example:

Start IDLE.

Navigate to the File menu and click New Window.

Type the following:

*Square of 3 in Python will be 3**2*

*Cube of 5 in Python will be 5**3*

- Square of 3

Start IDLE.

Navigate to the File menu and click New Window.

Type the following:

number=3   #declaring   variable   number   and
assigning value 3

square=number**2

print(square)   #Calling the print function to display
what square has

- Cube of 5

Start IDLE.

Navigate to the File menu and click New Window.

Type the following:

number=5   #declaring variable number and assigning
value 5

cube=number**3

print(cube)   #Calling the print function to display what
cube has

Practice Exercise

Use python operators to write and run a python program that find the following:

> ➢ Cube of 7
> ➢ Square of 15
> ➢ Cube of 6
> ➢ Square of 11
> ➢ Cube of 8
> ➢ Square of 13

Note: We can still multiply 2 two times to get the square of 2. The reason for using the square and cube operators is to help us write compact and efficient code. Remember that the interpreter goes through each line including comments only that it ignores comments. Using the cube and square operators helps compact code and increase the efficiency of interpretation including troubleshooting as well as human readability of the code.

Operators with String in Python

In Python programming language certain operators are used to help concatenate strings. The addition sign is used to concatenate strings in Python.

Example

Start IDLE.

Navigate to the File menu and click New Window.

Type the following:

status="I am happy I know" + "how to write programs in Python"

print(status)

Python Multiplication of a string to create a sequence

many_words="Great Programmer" * 5

print(many_words)

Practice Exercise

- ✓ Use a concatenation operator to join the following strings in Python

I have realized

that programming is passion,

dedication and frequent practice.

✓ Use an operator to generate ten times the following string

Happy

Summary

We have covered what constitutes variables in Python. Variables are named storage locations and for this reason, we have variable names. There are numerical and string variables. These are known as variable types. In handling variables and indeed any other aspect of Python we will encounter and use special words known as reserved words or keywords. Keywords are fixed and must be typed the way specified. Keywords cannot be used as variable names or identifiers. Comments (preceded using #,'" or """) are for human readability aspect of a Python program. Indentation is used in Python to group lines of codes into blocks. Different types of operators such as the arithmetic operators and string operators are used to allow for manipulation of variables supported by user and inbuilt functions in Python.

FIFTH DAY

Part 11: Python Sets

The attributes of a set are that it contains unique elements, the items are not ordered, and the elements are not changeable. The set itself can be changed.

Creating a set

Example

Start IDLE.

Navigate to the File menu and click New Window.

Type the following:

set_mine={5,6,7}

   print(set_mine)

set_yours={2.1,"Great",(7,8,9)}

   print(set_mine)

Creating a Set from a List

Example

Start IDLE.

Navigate to the File menu and click New Window.

Type the following:

set_mine=set([5,6,7,5])

   print(set_mine)

Practice Exercise

Start IDLE.

Navigate to the File menu and click New Window.

Type the following:

Correct and create a set in Python given the following set, trial_set={1,1,2,3,1,5,8,9}

Note

The {} will create a dictionary that is empty in Python. There is no need to index sets since they are ordered.

Adding elements to a set for multiple members we use the update() method.

For a single addition of a single element to a set we use the add() method. Duplicates should be avoided when handling sets.

Example

Start IDLE.

Navigate to the File menu and click New Window.

Type the following:

your_set={6,7}

print(your_set)

your_set.add(4)

print(your_set)

your_set.update([9,10,13])

print(your_set)

your_set.update([23, 37],{11,16,18})

print(your_set)

Removing Elements from a Set

The methods discard(o and remove() are used to purge an item from a set.

Example

Start IDLE.

Navigate to the File menu and click New Window.

Type the following:

set_mine={7,2,3,4,1}

print(set_mine)

set_mine.discard(2)

print(set_mine)   #Output will be {7,3,4,1}

set_mine.remove(1)

print(set_mine)   *#Output will be {7,3,4}*

Using the pop() Method to Remove an Item from a Set

Since sets are unordered, the order of popping items is arbitrary.

It is also possible to remove all items in a set using the clear() method in Python.

Start IDLE.

Navigate to the File menu and click New Window.

Type the following:

your_set=set("Today")

print(your_set)

print(your_set.pop())

your_set.pop()

print(your_set)

your_set.clear()

print(your_set)

Set Operations in Python

We use sets to compute difference, intersection, and union of sets.

Example

Start IDLE.

Navigate to the File menu and click New Window.

Type the following:

C={5,6,7,8,9,11}

D={6,9,11,13,15}

Set Union

A union of sets C and D will contain both sets' elements.

In Python the| operator generates a union of sets. The union() will also generate a union of sets.

Example

Start IDLE.

Navigate to the File menu and click New Window.

Type the following:

C={5,6,7,8,9,11}

D={6,9,11,13,15}

print(C|D)   #Output: {5,6,7,8,9,11,13,15}

Example 2

Using the union()

Start IDLE.

Navigate to the File menu and click New Window.

Type the following:

C={5,6,7,8,9,11}

D={6,9,11,13,15}

print(D.union(C))   #Output:{5,6,7,8,9,11,13,15}

Practice Exercise

Rewrite the following into a set and find the set union.

A={1,1,2,3,4,4,5,12,14,15}

D={2,3,3,7,8,9,12,15}

Set Intersection

A and D refers to a new items set that are shared by both sets. The & operator is used to perform intersection. The intersection() function can also be used to intersect sets.

Example

Start IDLE.

Navigate to the File menu and click New Window.

Type the following:

A = {11, 12, 13, 14, 15}

D= {14, 15,16, 17, 18}

Print(A&D)   #Will display {14,15}

Using intersection()

Example

Start IDLE.

Navigate to the File menu and click New Window.

Type the following:

A = {11, 12, 13, 14, 15}

D= {14, 15,16, 17, 18}

A.intersection(D)

Set Difference

A-D refers to a new items set are only in A but not in D. In the same way, D-A is a set of element in D but not in A. The − operator is used to compute the difference. The difference() method can also be used.

Example 1

Start IDLE.

Navigate to the File menu and click New Window.

Type the following:

A = {11, 12, 13, 14, 15}

D= {14, 15,16, 17, 18}

print(A - D)   *#Output:{11,12,13}*

Example 2

Start IDLE.

Navigate to the File menu and click New Window.

Type the following:

A = {11, 12, 13, 14, 15}

D= {14, 15,16, 17, 18}

print(A.difference(D))

Example 3

A = {11, 12, 13, 14, 15}

D= {14, 15,16, 17, 18}

Print(D-A)   *#Output will be {18,16,17}*

Set Symmetric Difference

The set of elements in both A and D except those that are common in both is known as the symmetric difference of A and D. The ^ operator is used to perform symmetric difference and the same can also be attained using the symmetric difference() operator.

Example 1

Start IDLE.

Navigate to the File menu and click New Window.

Type the following:

A = {11, 12, 13, 14, 15}

D= {14, 15,16, 17, 18}

print (A^D)   #Output:{11,12,13,16,17,18)

Example 2

A = {11, 12, 13, 14, 15}

D= {14, 15,16, 17, 18}

print(A.symmetric_difference(D)   #Output:{11,12,13,16,17,18)

Challenge: Is A^D and D^A the same?

Example: Adding elements in a Set

Paint_set = set()

paint_set.add("brown")

print(paint_set)

paint_set.update(["white", "violet"])

print(paint_set)

Superset and Subset

Start IDLE.

Navigate to the File menu and click New Window.

Type the following:

set1 = set(["A", "M"])

set2 = set(["M", "O"])

set3 = set(["M"])

issubset = set1 <= set2

print(issubset)

issuperset = set1 >= set1

print(issuperset)

issubset = set3 <= set2

print(issubset)

issuperset = set2 >= set3

print(issuperset)

Membership Tests in Sets

Example

Start IDLE.

Navigate to the File menu and click New Window.

Type the following:

set_mine = set("pawpaw")

print('p' in set_mine)

Iteration

Python commonly employs the for control statement to continually scan a set.

Example

Start IDLE.

Navigate to the File menu and click New Window.

Type the following:

for letter in set("pawpaw")

  print(letter)

Inbuilt Functions with Set

Frozenset Python

Just like tuples are immutable. frozensets are immutable. To create frozensets we use the function frozenset().

Example

Start IDLE.

Navigate to the File menu and click New Window.

Type the following:

A = frozenset([11, 12, 13, 14])

D = frozenset([13, 14, 15, 16])

Summary

Set in **Python** is a data structure equivalent to **sets** in mathematics. It may consist of various elements; the order of elements in a **set** is undefined. You can add and delete elements of a **set**, you can iterate the elements of the **set**, you can perform standard operations on **sets** (union, intersection, difference).

Part 12: Python Dictionaries

While many things in Python are iterables, not all of them are sequences and a Python dictionary falls in this category. In this article, we will talk about what a Python dictionary is, how it works, and what are its most common applications.

What is a Python Dictionary?

Getting clean and actionable data is one of the key challenges in data analysis. You can't build and fit models to data that isn't usable. A Python dictionary makes it easier to read and change data, thereby rendering it more actionable for predictive modeling.

A Python dictionary holds a key: value pair. The Python dictionary is optimized in a manner that allows it to access values when the key is known.

While each key is separated by a comma in a Python Dictionary, each key-value pair is separated by a colon. Moreover, while the keys of the dictionary have to be unique and immutable (tuples, strings, integers, etcetera), the key-values can be of any type and can also be repeated any number of times. An example of a Python dictionary is shown below:

How do Python Dictionaries Work?

While there are several Python dictionary methods, there are some basic operations that need to be mastered. We will walk through the most important ones in this section.

Creating a Python dictionary

To create a Python dictionary you need to put items (each having a key and a corresponding value expressed as key: value) inside curly brackets. Each item needs to be separated from the next by a comma. As discussed above, values can repeat and be of any type. Keys, on the other hand, are unique and immutable. There is also a built-in function dict() that you can use to create a dictionary. For easier understanding note that this built in function is written as diction() in the rest of this book. Here are some examples:

Accessing Items within the Python dictionary

Accessing items in the dictionary in Python is simple enough. All you need to do is put the key name of the item within square brackets. This is important because the keys are unique and non-repeatable.

Example

To get the value of the model key:

k = thisdiction["model"]

You can also use another of the Python dictionary methods get() to access the item. Here's what it looks like.

k = thisdiction.get("model")

How to Change Values in a Python Dictionary

To change the value of an item, you once again need to refer to the key name. Here is an example.

If you have to change the value for the key "year" from 1890 to 2025:

thisdiction = {

"brand": "Mitsubishi",

"model": "Toyota",

"year": 1890

}

thisdiction["year"] = 2025

How Do You Loop Through a Python Dictionary

You can use a for loop function to loop through a dictionary in Python. By default, the return value while looping through the dictionary will be the keys of the dictionary. However, there are other methods that can be used to return the values.

To print the key names:

```
for k in thisdiction:
```

```
print(k)
```

To print the values in the dictionary, one by one:

```
for k in thisdiction:
```

```
print(thisdiction[k])
```

Another way of returning the values by using the values() function :

```
for k in thisdiction.values():
```

```
print(k)
```

If you want to Loop through both the keys and the values, you can use the items() function:

```
for k, m in thisdiction.items():
```

```
print(k, m)
```

How Do You Check if a Key Exists in the Dictionary

Here's how you can determine whether a particular key is actually present in the Python dictionary:

Say you have to check whether the key "model" is present in the dictionary:

thisdiction = {

"brand": "Mitsubishi",

"model": "Toyota",

"year": 1890

}

if "model" in thisdiction:

print("Yes, 'model' is one of the keys in the thisdiction dictionary")

How Do You Determine the Number of Items in the Dictionary

To determine the number of key: value pairs in the dictionary we use one of the most commonly used Python Dictionary methods, len(). Here's how it works:

print(len(thisdiction))

How to add an item to the Python Dictionary

To add a new key: value pair to the dictionary, you have to use a new index key and then assign a value to it.

For instance,

thisdiction = {

"brand": "Mitsubishi",

"model": "Toyota",

"year": 1890

}

thisdiction["color"] = "pink"

print(thisdiction)

Removing Items from the Python Dictionary

Here are some of the methods to remove an item from the Python dictionary. Each approaches the same goal from a different perspective.

Method 1

This method, pop(), removes the item which has the key name that is being specified. This works well since key names are unique and immutable.

thisdiction = {

"brand": "Mitsubishi",

"model": "Toyota",

"year": 1890

}

thisdiction.pop("model")

print(thisdiction)

Method 2

The popitem() method removes the item that has been added most recently. In earlier versions, this method used to remove any random item. Here's how it works:

thisdiction = {

"brand": "Mitsubishi",

"model": "Toyota",

"year": 1890

}

thisdiction.popitem()

print(thisdiction)

Method 3

Much like the pop() method, the del keyword removes the item whose key name has been mentioned.

thisdiction = {

"brand": "Mitsubishi",

"model": "Toyota",

"year": 1890

}

del thisdiction["model"]

print(thisdiction)

Method 4

Unlike the pop() method, the del keyword can also be used to delete the dictionary altogether. Here's how it can be used to do so:

thisdiction = {

"brand": "Mitsubishi",

"model": "Toyota",

"year": 1890

}

del thisdiction

print(thisdiction) #this will cause an error because "thisdiction" no longer exists.

Method 5

The clear() keyword empties the dictionary of all items without deleting the dictionary itself:

thisdiction = {

"brand": "Mitsubishi",

"model": "Toyota",

"year": 1890

}

thisdiction.clear()

print(thisdiction)

A list of Common Python Dictionary Methods

There are a number of Python Dictionary methods that can be used to perform basic operations. Here is a list of the most commonly used ones.

Method	Description
clear()	This removes all the items from the dictionary
copy()	This method returns a copy of the Python dictionary
fromkeys()	This returns a different directory with only the key : value pairs that have been specified
get()	This returns the value of the key mentioned
items()	This method returns the thuple for every key: value pair in the dictionary

keys()	This returns a list of all the Python dictionary keys in the dictionary
popitem()	In the latest version, this method deletes the most recently added item
pop()	This removes only the key that is mentioned
update()	This method updates the dictionary with certain key-value pairs that are mentioned
values()	This method simply returns the values of all the items in the list

Merits of a Dictionary in Python

Here are some of the major pros of a Python library:

- It improves the readability of your code. Writing out Python dictionary keys along with values adds a layer of documentation to the code. If the code is more streamlined, it is a lot easier to debug. Ultimately, analyses get done a lot quicker and models can be fitted more efficiently.

- Apart from readability, there's also the question of sheer speed. You can look up a key in a Python dictionary very fast. The speed of a task like looking up keys is measured by looking at how many operations it takes to finish. Looking up a key is done in constant time compared with looking up an item in a large list which is done in linear time.

To look up an item in a huge list, the computer will look through every item in the list. If every item is assigned a key-value pair then you only need to look for the key which makes the entire process much faster. A Python dictionary is basically an implementation of a hash table. Therefore, it has all the benefits of the hash table which include membership checks and speedy tasks like looking up keys.

Demerits of a Python dictionary

While a Python dictionary is easily one of the most useful tools, especially for data cleaning and data analysis, it does have a downside. Here are some demerits of using a Python dictionary.

✓ Dictionaries are unordered. In cases where the order of the data is important, the Python dictionary is not appropriate.

✓ Python dictionaries take up a lot more space than other data structures. The amount of space occupied increases drastically when there are many Python Dictionary keys. Of course, this isn't too much of a disadvantage because memory isn't very expensive.

Data Structures in Python

Among the basic data types and structures in Python are the following:

- Logical: bool

- Numeric: int, float, complex

- Sequence: list, tuple, range

- Text Sequence: str

- Binary Sequence: bytes, bytearray, memoryview

- Map: dict

- Set: set, frozenset

All of the above are classes from which object instances can be created. In addition to the above, more data types/structures are available in modules that come as part of any default Python installation: collections, heapq, array, enum, etc. Extra numeric types are available from modules numbers, decimals and fractions. The built-in function type() allows us to obtain the type of any object.

Discussion

- With respect to data types, what are the differences between Python2 and Python3?

  The following are important differences:

- A division such as 5 / 2 returns integer value 2 in Python2 due to truncation. In Python3, this will evaluate to float value 2.5 even when the input values are only integers.

- In Python2, strings were ASCII. To use Unicode, one had to use the unicode type by creating them with a prefix: name = u'Saṃsāra'. In Python3, str type is Unicode by default.

- Python2 has int and long types but both these are integrated in Python3 as int. Integers can be as large as system memory allows.

- **What data structures in Python are immutable and mutable?**

  Mutable objects are those that can be changed after they are created, such as updating/adding/removing an element in a list. It can be said that mutable objects are changed in place.

  Immutable objects can't be changed in place after they are created. Among the immutable basic data types/structures
  are bool, int, float, complex, str, tuple, range, frozenset, and bytes.
  The mutable counterparts
  of frozenset and bytes are set and bytearray respectively.
  Among the other mutable data structures
  are list and dict.
  With immutable objects it may seem like we can modify their values by assignment. What actually happens is that a new immutable object is created and then assigned to the existing variable. This can be verified by checking the ID (using id() function) of the variable before and after assignment.

- **What data structures in Python are suited to handle binary data?**

The fundamental built-in types for manipulating binary data are bytearray and bytes. They support memoryview that makes use of the buffer protocol to access the storage location of other binary objects without making a copy.

The module array supports storage of simple data types such as thirty-two-bit integers and double floating point values. Characters, integers and floats can be stored array types, which gives low-level access to the bytes that store the data.

- **What containers and sequences are available in Python?**

The diagram below shows List data type and its relationship to other data types.

Containers are data structures that contain one or more objects. In Python, a container object can contain objects of different types. For that matter, a container can contain other containers at any depth. Containers may also be called **collections.**

Sequences are containers that have inherent ordering among their items. For example, a string such as str = "hello world" is a sequence of Unicode characters h, e, l, etc. Note that there is no character data type in Python, and the expression "h" is actually a 1-character string.

Sequences support two main operations (for example, sequence variable seq):

- Indexing: Access a particular element: seq[0] (first element), seq[-1] (last element).

- Slicing: Access a subset of elements with syntax seq[start:stop:step]: seq[0::2] (alternate elements), seq[0:3] (first three elements), seq[-3:] (last three elements). Note that the stop point is not included in the result.

Among the basic sequence types are list, tuple, range, str, bytes bytearray and memoryvie w. Conversely, dict, set and frozenset are simply containers in which elements don't have any particular order. More containers are part of collections module.

- **How can I construct some common containers?**

The following examples are self-explanatory:

- str: a = '' (empty), a = "" (empty), a = 'Hello'
- bytes: a = b'' (empty), a = b"" (empty), a = b'Hello'

- list: a = list() (empty), a = [] (empty), a = [1, 2, 3]
- tuple: a = tuple() (empty), a = (1,) (single item), a = (1, 2, 3), a = 1, 2, 3
- set: a = set() (empty), a = {1, 2, 3}
- dict: a = dict() (empty), a = {} (empty), a = {1:2, 2:4, 3:9}

We can
construct bytearray from bytes and frozenset from set usi
ng their respective built-in functions.

- **What are iterables and iterators?**

An iterable is a container that can be processed element by element. For sequences, elements are processed in the order they are stored. For non-sequences, elements are processed in some arbitrary order.

Formally, any object that implements the **iterator protocol** is an iterable. The iterator protocol is defined by two special methods, __iter__() and __next__(). Calling iter() on an iterable returns what is called an iterator. Calling next() on an iterator gives us the next element of the iterable. Thus, iterators help us process the iterable element by element.

When we use loops or comprehensions in Python, iterators are used under the hood. Programmers don't need to call iter() or next() explicitly.

- **Can I convert from one data type to another?**

  Yes, provided they are compatible. Here are some examples:

- int('3') will convert from string to integer

- int(3.4) will truncate float to integer

- bool(0) and bool([]) will both return False

- ord('A') will return the equivalent Unicode code point as an integer value

- chr(65) will return the equivalent Unicode string of one character

- bin(100), oct(100) and hex(100) will return string representations in their respective bases

- int('45', 16) and int('0x45', 16) will convert from hexadecimal to decimal

- tuple([1, 2, 3]) will convert from list to tuple

- list('hello') will split the string into a list of 1-character strings

- set([1, 1, 2, 3]) will remove duplicates in the list to give a set

- dict([(1,2), (2,4), (3,9)]) will construct a dictionary from the given list of tuples

- list({1:2, 2:4, 3:9}) will return a list based on the dictionary keys.

- **Should I use a list or a tuple?**

If ordering is important, sets and dictionaries should not be used: prefer lists and tuples. Tuples are used to pass arguments and return results from functions. This is because they can contain multiple elements and are immutable. Tuples are also good for storing closely related data. For example, (a, b, c) coordinates or (red, green, blue) color components can be stored as tuples. Use lists instead if values can change during the lifetime of the object.

If a sequence is to be sorted, use a list for in-place sorting. A tuple can be used but it should return a new sorted object. A tuple cannot be sorted in-place.

For better code readability, elements of a tuple can be named. For this purpose, use collections.namedtuple class. This allows us to access the elements via their names rather than tuple indices.

It's possible to convert between lists and tuples using functions list() and tuple().

- **When to use a set and when to use a dict?**

Sets and dictionaries have no order. However, from Python 3.7, the order in which items are inserted into a dict are preserved.

Sets store unique items. Duplicates are discarded. Dictionaries can contain duplicate values but keys must be unique. Since dict keys are unique, often dict is used for counting. For example, to count the number of times a word appears in a document, words can be keys and counts can be values.

Sets are suited for finding the intersection/union of two groups, such as finding those who live in a neighborhood (set 1) and/or also own a car (set 2). Other set operations are also possible.

Strings, lists and tuples can take only integers as indices due to their ordered nature but dictionaries can be indexed by strings as well. In general, dictionaries can be indexed by any of the built-in immutable types, which are considered **hashable.** Thus, dictionaries are suited for key-value pairs such as mapping country names (keys) to their capitals (values). But if capitals are the more common input to your algorithm, use them as keys instead.

- **How can I implement a linked list in Python?**

Linked list is a group of nodes connected by pointers or links. **A node** is one point of statistics or details in the linked list. Not only does it hold data but also it shows direction to the following node in a linked list that is single. Thus, the definition of a node is recursive. For a double-linked list, the node has two pointers, one that connects to the previous node and another one that connects to the next node. Linked lists can be designed to be ordered or unordered.

The head of the linked list must be accessible. This allows us to traverse the entire list and perform all possible operations. A double-linked list might also expose the tail for traversal from the end. While a Node class may be enough to implement a linked list, it's common to encapsulate the head pointer and all operations within LinkedList class. Operations on the linked lists are methods of the class. One possible implementation is given by Downey. A DoubleLinkedList can be a derived class from LinkedList with the addition of a tail pointer and associated methods.

Dictionary

When the key is known dictionaries will retrieve values.

Creating a Dictionary

A dictionary is generated by having items in curly braces demarcated by a comma. A dictionary element has a key and a matching value. The key and value in Python are captured as a pair. Normally, key: value. Keys have to be immutable and unique.

Example

Start IDLE.

Navigate to the File menu and click New Window.

Type the following:

dict_mine= {}   *#Empty dictionary*

 # dictionary with integer keys

dict_mine= {2: 'pawpaw', 4: 'rectangle'}   *#dictionary with integer keys*

dict_mine = {'student': 'Brenda',2:[12, 14, 13]}#dictionary with integer keys

dict_mine = dict({2:'student': 'Brenda'})

dict_mine = dict([(2, 'pawpaw'), (4, 'rectangle')])

Accessing Elements from a Dictionary

Dictionary uses keys instead of indexing to access values. The keys can be within the square brackets or with the get() method.

Example

Start IDLE.

Navigate to the File menu and click New Window.

Type the following:

dict_mine = {'name':'James', 'age': 62}

print(dict_mine['name'])

print(dict_mine.get('age'))

Add or Modify Dictionary Elements

For dictionaries, they are mutable implying that we can modify the value of current items using the assignment operator. The value will get updated if the key is already existing else we will have to add new key: the dictionary value couple.

Start IDLE.

Navigate to the File menu and click New Window.

Type the following:

dict_mine={'student':'James','age':62}

dict_mine['age'] = 37

print(dict_mine)

dict_mine['address'] = 'New York'

print(dict_mine)

Removing/Deleting Elements from a Dictionary

Example

Start IDLE.

Navigate to the File menu and click New Window.

Type the following:

my_squares={10:100,8:64,12:224}

print(my_squares.pop(2))

print(my_squares)

print(my_squares.popitem())

print(my_squares)

del my_squares[4]

print(my_squares)

my_squares.clear()

print(squares)

del my_squares

Dictionary Methods in Python

Example

Start IDLE.

Navigate to the File menu and click New Window.

Type the following:

```
scores ={}.fromkeys(['Chemistry','Spanish','Pyschology'], 0)

print(scores)

for item in marks.items():

    print(item)
```

Start IDLE.

Navigate to the File menu and click New Window.

Type the following:

```
list(sorted(scores.keys()))
```

Dictionary Comprehension in Python

```
my_squares = {y: y*y for y in range(5)}
```

print(my_squares)

Alternatively, the program can be written as:

my_power = {}

for y in range(5):

   power[y] = y*y

Odd Items Only Dictionary

Example

Start IDLE.

Navigate to the File menu and click New Window.

Type the following:

squares_odd={y:y*y for y in range(10) if y%2==1}

print(squares_odd)

Membership Test in a Dictionary

Using the keyword in, we can evaluate if a key is in a particular dictionary. The membership tests should be used for dictionary keys and not for dictionary values.

Example

Start IDLE.

Navigate to the File menu and click New Window.

Type the following:

my_squares = {10: 100, 6: 36, 8: 64, 11: 121}

print(11 in my_squares)

print(36 in squares)

Practice Exercise

Given:

square_dict={2:4,6:36,8:64}

- Use membership to test if 6 exist in the dictionary.
- Use membership, test if 36 exist in the dictionary.

Iteration in a Dictionary

We use the for loop to iterate through each key in a particular dictionary.

Inbuilt Functions

Example

Start IDLE.

Navigate to the File menu and click New Window.

Type the following:

your_squares = {2: 4, 4: 16, 6: 36, 8: 64, 10: 100}

print(len(your_squares))

print(sorted(your_squares))

for i in squares:

   print(your_squares[i])

Practice Exercise

Give the following set, setm=set(["Blue","Yellow"])

- ✓ Write a working program to copy the set elements.
- ✓ Display the new set.
- ✓ Clear the set.
- ✓ Print the latest status of the set.

Given the setr=set(["Knock","Up"])

- ✓ Write a simple program to copy the set elements.
- ✓ Write a working program to display the latest status of the set.
- ✓ Write a simple program clear the elements of the set.
- ✓ Display the latest status of the set.
- ✓ Delete the entire set using del.

Given m=frozenset([11,12,13,14,15]) and n=([13,14,15,16,17])

- ❖ Use the isdisjoint() to test of the sets have no shared elements.
- ❖ Write a program to return a new set with items in the set that are not in the others.
- ❖ Write a union of sets m and n.
- ❖ Write an intersection of sets n and m.
- ❖ Write a program to pop an item in set n.

❖ Write a program that appends element 21 to the set m.

❖ Check to see if set m has element 14 using a built-in keyword.

❖ Use discard() to drop all items in the set m.

Given this set second_set = {"berry", "pineaple", "melon"}

❖ Write a Python program to update the set with these elements at a go "mango","guava", "plum"

❖ Find the length of this set using the len().

❖ Use remove() to clear the set.

Given {(, 17, 19, 21)

❖ Use set constructor set() to construct a set named third_set in Python.

❖ Use the add() method to add "Kim" to the set.

❖ Pop an element from the set using pop().

❖ Update the set using update() to include {43,41,40}

Given setq=([13,2,17,8,19])

❖ Find the minimum value in the set using inbuilt features of Python.

❖ Find the maximum value in the set using inbuilt features of Python.

Given setb=([5,"K", 8, 1])

❖ Use the for a statement to write a Python program that iterates through the set elements.

Given

diction1={11:12,12:27}

diction2={13:52,13:57}

❖ Create a python program to concatenate the dictionaries in one.

Summary

At the end of the day, a Python dictionary represents a data structure that can prove valuable in cleaning data and making it actionable. It becomes even more valuable because it is inherently simple to use and much faster and more efficient as well. Of course, if you are looking for a career in data science, a comprehensive course with live sessions, assessments, and placement assistance might be just what you need.

In python, the attributes of a set include having items that are not ordered, items that are unique and each element in a set is unchangeable. Adding elements to a set for multiple members we use the update() method. For a single addition of a single element to a set, we use the add() method. Duplicates should be avoided when handling sets. Using the keyword in, we can evaluate if a key is in a particular dictionary. The membership tests should be used for keys and not for values.

SIXTH DAY

Part 13: Object-Oriented Programming in Python

Object and Class in Python

Python supports different programming approaches as it is a multi-paradigm. An object in Python has an attribute and behavior.

Example

Car as an object:

Attributes: color, mileage, model, age.

Behavior: reverse, speed, turn, roll, stop, start.

Class

It is a template for creating an object.

Example

class Car:

NOTE:

By convention, we write the class name with the first letter as uppercase. A class name is in singular form by convention.

Syntax

class Name_of_Class:

From a class, we can construct objects by simply making an instance of the class. The class_name() operator creates an object by assigning the object to the empty method.

Object/Class Instantiation

From our class Car, we can have several objects such as a first car, second care or SUVs.

Example

Start IDLE.

Navigate to the File menu and click New Window.

Type the following:

my_car=Car()

   pass

Practice Exercise

- ✓ Create a class and an object for students.
- ✓ Create a class and an object for the hospital.
- ✓ Create a class and an object for a bank.
- ✓ Create a class and an object for a police department.

Example

Start IDLE.

Navigate to the File menu and click New Window.

Type the following:

```
class Car:

category="Personal Automobile"

   def __init__(self, model, insurance):

      self.model = model

      self.insurance =insurance

subaru=Car("Subaru","Insured")

toyota=Car("Toyota","Uninsured")

print("Subaru is a {}".format(subaru._class_.car))

print("Toyota is a {}".format(toyota._class_.car))

print("{} is {}".format(subaru.model, subaru.insurance))

print("{} is {}".format(toyota.model, toyota.insurance))
```

Methods

Functions defined within a body of the class are known as methods and are basic functions. Methods define the behaviors of an object.

Example

Start IDLE.

Navigate to the File menu and click New Window.

Type the following:

```
def __init__(self, model, insurance):

    self.model = model

    self.insurance =insurance

  def ignite(self, ignite):

    return "{} ignites {}".format(self.model, ignition)

  def stop(self):

    return "{} is now stopping".format(self.model)

subaru=Car("Subaru","Insured")

print(subaru.ignite("'Fast'"))

print(subaru.stop())
```

NOTE

The methods ignite() and stop() are referred to as instance methods because they are an instance of the object created.

Practice Exercise

- ✓ Create a class Dog and instantiate it.
- ✓ Create a Python program to show names of two dogs and their two attributes from a.

Inheritance

A way of creating a new class by using details of existing class devoid of modifying it is called inheritance. The derived class or child class is the newly formed class while the existing class is called parent or base class.

Example

Start IDLE.

Navigate to the File menu and click New Window.

Type the following:

```python
class Dog:

    def __init__(self):

        print("Dog is available")

    def whoisThis(self):

        print("Dog")

    def walk(self):

        print("Walks gently")

class Spitz(Dog):        #Child class

    def __init__(self):

        super().__init__()

        print("Spitz is now available")

    def whoisThis(self):

        print("Pitbull")

    def wag(self):

        print("Strong")

pitbull = Pitbull()
```

pitbull.whoisThis()

pitbull.walk()

pitbull.wag()

Discussion

We created two Python classes in the program above. The classes were Dog as the base class and Pitbull as the derived class. The derived class inherits the functions of the base class. The method _init_() and the function super() are used to pull the content of _init_() method from the base class into the derived class.

Encapsulation in Python

Encapsulation in Python Object Oriented Programming approach is meant to help prevent data from direct modification. Private attributes in Python are denoted using a single or double underscore as a prefix.

Example

Start IDLE.

Navigate to the File menu and click New Window.

Type the following:

"__" or "_".

```
class Tv:

    def __init__(self):

        self.__Finalprice = 800

    def offer(self):

        print("Offering Price: {}".format(self.__finalprice))

    def set_final_price(self, offer):

        self.__finalprice = offer

t = Tv()

t.offer()

t.__finalprice = 950

t.offer()

# using setter function

t.setFinalPrice(990)

t.sell()
```

Discussion

The program defined a class Tv and used _init_(o methods to hold the final offering price of the TV. Along the way, we attempted to change the price but could not manage. The reason for the inability to change is because Python treated the _finalprice as private attributes. The only way to modify this value was through using a setter function, setMaxPrice() that takes price as a parameter.

Polymorphism

In Python, polymorphism refers to the ability to use a shared interface for several data types.

Start IDLE.

Navigate to the File menu and click New Window.

Type the following:

class Tilapia:

  def swim(self):

    print("Tilapia can swim")

  def fly(self):

```
    print("Tilapia cannot fly")

class Shark:

    def jump(self):

    print("Shark can't fly")

    def swim(self):

    print("Shark can swim")

def jumping_test(fish):

    fish.jump()

bonny = Tilapia()

biggy = Shark()

jumping_test(bonny)

jumping_test(biggy)
```

Discussion

The program above has defined two classes Tilapia and Shark all of which share the method jump() even though they have different functions. By creating common interface jumping_test() we allowed polymorphism in the program above. We then passed objects bonny and biggy in the jumping_test() function.

Practice Exercise

- ✓ In a doctor consultation room suggest the class and objects in a programming context.
- ✓ In a football team, suggest programming class and objects.
- ✓ In a grocery store, suggest programming class and objects.

Class Definition in Python

The keyword def is used to define a class in Python. The first string in a Python class is used to describe the class even though it is not always needed.

Example

Start IDLE.

Navigate to the File menu and click New Window.

Type the following:

class Dog

'''Briefly taking about class Dog using this docstring'''

Pass

Example 2

Start IDLE.

Navigate to the File menu and click New Window.

Type the following:

Class Bright:

"My other class"

b=10

def salute(self):

print('Welcome')

print(Bright.b)

print(Bright.salute)

print(Bright.__doc__)

Object Creation in Python

Example from the previous class

Open the previous program file with class Bright

student1=Bright()

Discussion

The last program will create object student1, a new instance. The attributes of objects can be accessed via the specific object name prefix. The attributes can be a method or data including the matching class functions. In other terms, Bright.salute is a function object and student1.salute will be a method object.

Example

Start IDLE.

Navigate to the File menu and click New Window.

Type the following:

class Bright:

  "Another class again!"

  c = 20

```
def salute(self):

    print('Hello')

student2 = Bright()

print(Bright.salute)

print(student2.salute)

student2.salute()
```

Discussion

We invoked the student2.salute() despite the parameter 'self' and it still worked without placing arguments. The reason for this phenomenon is because each time an object calls its method, the object itself is passed as the first argument. The implication is that student2.salute() translates into student2.salute(student2). It is the reason for the 'self; name.

Constructors

Start IDLE.

Navigate to the File menu and click New Window.

Type the following:

```python
class NumberComplex

class ComplexNumber:

    def __init__(self,realnum = 0,i = 0):

        self.real = realnum

        self.imaginarynum = i

    def getData(self):

        print("{0}+{1}j".format(self.realnumber,self.imaginarynum))

complex1 = NumberComplex(2,3)

complex1.getData()

complex2 = NumberComplex(5)

complex2.attribute = 10

print((complex2.realnumber, complex2.imaginarynumber, complex2.attribute))

complex1.attribute
```

Deleting Objects and Attributes

The del statement is used to delete attributes of an object at any instance.

Example

Start IDLE.

Navigate to the File menu and click New Window.

Type the following:

complex1 = NumberComplex(2,3)

del complex1.imaginarynumber

complex1.getData()

del NumberComplex.getData

complex1.getData()

Deleting the Entire Object

Example

Start IDLE.

211

Navigate to the File menu and click New Window.

Type the following:

complex1=NumberComplex(1,3)

del complex1

Discussion

When complex1=NumberComplex(1,3) is done, a new instance of the object gets generated in memory and the name complex1 ties with it. The object does not immediately get destroyed as it temporarily stays in memory before the garbage collector purges it from memory. The purging of the object helps free resources bound to the object and enhances system efficiency. Garbage destruction Python refers to automatic destruction of unreferenced objects.

Inheritance in Python

In Python inheritance allows us to specify a class that takes all the functionality from the base class and adds more. It is a powerful feature of OOP.

Syntax

class ParentClass:

  Body of parent class

class ChildClass(ParentClass):

  Body of derived class

Example

Start IDLE.

Navigate to the File menu and click New Window.

Type the following:

class Rect_mine(Rect_mine):

  def __init__(self):

    Shape.__init__(self,4)

  def getArea(self):

    s1, s2, s3,s4 = self.count_sides

    perimeter = (s1+s2+s3+s4)

area = (s1*s2)

print('The rectangle area is:' %area)

Example 2

r = rect_mine()

r.inputSides()

Type b1 : 4

Type l1 : 8

Type b2 : 4

Type l1:   8

r.dispSides()

Type b1 is 4.0

Type l1 is 8.0

Type b2 is 4.0

Type l1 is 8.0

r.getArea()

Method Overriding in Python

When a method is defined in both the base class and the derived class, the method in the child class/derived class will override the parent/base class. In the above example, _init_() method in Rectangle class will override the _init_() in Shape class.

Inheritance in Multiple Form in Python

Example

Start IDLE.

Navigate to the File menu and click New Window.

Type the following:

In this case, MultiInherit is derived from class Parent1 and Parent2.

Multilevel Inheritance

Inheriting from a derived class is called multilevel inheritance.

Example

Start IDLE.

Navigate to the File menu and click New Window.

Type the following:

class Parent:

  pass

class Multilevel1(Parent):

  pass

class Multilevel2(Multilevel1):

  pass

Discussion

Multilevel1 derives from Parent, and Multilevel2 derives from Multilevel1.

Method Resolution Order

Example

Start IDLE.

Navigate to the File menu and click New Window.

Type the following:

print(issubclass(list,object))

print(isinstance(6.7,object))

print(isinstance("Welcome",object))

Discussion

The particular attribute in a class will be scanned first. The search will continue into parent classes. This search does not repeat searching the same class twice. The approach or order of searching is sometimes called linearization of multiderived class in Python. The Method Resolution Order refers to the rules needed to determine this order.

Operator Overloading

Inbuilt classes can use operators and the same operators will behave differently with different types. An example is the + that depending on context will perform concatenation of two strings, arithmetic addition on numbers, or merge lists. Operating overloading is an OOP feature that allows assigning varying meaning to an operator subject to context.

Making Class Compatible with Inbuilt Special Functions

Example

Start IDLE.

Navigate to the File menu and click New Window.

Type the following:

```
class Planar:

    def __init__(self, x_axis= 0, y_axis = 0):

        self.x_axis = x_axis

        self.y_axis = y_axis

    def __str__(self):

        return "({0},{1})".format(self.x_axis,self.y_axis)
```

Discussion

```
planar1=Planar(3,5)

print(planar1)          #The output will be (3,5)
```

Using More Inbuilt Methods

Example

Start IDLE.

Navigate to the File menu and click New Window.

Type the following:

```
class Planar:

    def __init__(self, x_axis= 0, y_axis = 0):

        self.x_axis = x_axis

        self.y_axis = y_axis

str(planar1)

format(planar1)
```

Discussion

It then follows that each time we invoke format(planar1) or str(planar1), Python is in effect executing planar1._str_() thus the name, special functions.

Operator + Overloading

The _add_() function addition in a class will overload the +.

Example

Start IDLE.

Navigate to the File menu and click New Window.

Type the following:

class Planar:

  def __init__(self, x_axis= 0, y_axis = 0):

   self.x_axis = x_axis

   self.y_axis = y_axis

  def __str__(self):

   return "({0},{1})".format(self.x_axis,self.y_axis)

  def __add__(self,z):

   x_axis = self.x_axis + z.x_axis

   y_axis = self.y_axis + z.y_axis

return Planar(x_axis,y_axis)

Practice Exercise

- Print planar1 + planar2 from the example above.

Discussion

When you perform planar1+planar2 in Python, it will call planar._add_(planar2) and in turn Planar._add_(planar1, planar2).

Revisit Logical and Comparison Operators

Practice Exercise

- ❖ Given x=8, y=9, write a Python program that uses logical equals to test if x is equal to y.
- ❖ Write a program that evaluates x!=y in Python programming language.
- ❖ Write and run the following program

m = True

n = False

print('m and n is',m and n)

print('m or n is',m or n)

print('not m is',not n)

❖ From the program in c., which program statement(s) evaluates to True, or False.

❖ Write and run the following program in Python

```
m1 = 15

n1 = 15

m2 = 'Welcome'

n2 = 'Welcome'

m3 = [11,12,13]

n3 = [11,12,13]

print(m1 is not n1)

print(m2 is n2)

print(m3 is n3)
```

❖ Which program statement(s) generate True or False states in e.

❖ Write and run the following program

```
m = 'Welcome'
```

n = {11:'b',12:'c'}

print('W' in m)

print('Welcome' not in m)

print(10 in n)

print('b' in n)

❖ Which program statement(s) in g. return True or False states.

The special functions needed for overloading other operators are listed below.

Comparison Operators Overloading

In Python, comparison operators can be overloaded.

Example

class Planar:

   def __init__(self, x_axis= 0, y_axis = 0):

   self.x_axis = x_axis

   self.y_axis = y_axis

def __str__(self):

  return "({0},{1})".format(x_axis,y_axis)

def __lt__(self,z):

  self_magnitude = (x_axis ** 3) + (y_axis ** 3)

  z_magnitude = (z.x_axis ** 3) + (z.y_axis ** 3)

  return self_magnitude < z_magnitude

Practice Exercise

a. Perform the following to the example above Planar(1,1)

b. Again perform Planar(1,1) in the above example.

c. Finally, perform Planar(1,1) from the above example.

Summary

Python supports different programming approaches as it is a multi-paradigm. An object in Python has an attribute and behavior. From a class, we can construct objects by simply making an instance of the class. The class_name() operator creates an object by assigning the object to the empty method. The keyword def is used to define a class in Python. The first string in a Python class is used to describe the class even though it is not always needed. When a method is defined in both the base class and the derived class, the method in the child class/derived class will override the parent/base class. In the above example, _init_() method in Rectangle class will override the _init_() in Shape class.

Inbuilt classes can use operators and the same operators will behave differently with different types. An example is the + that depending on context will perform concatenation of two strings, arithmetic addition on numbers, or merge lists. Operating overloading is an OOP feature that allows assigning varying meaning to an operator subject to context.From a class, we can construct objects by simply making an instance of the class. The class_name() operator creates an object by assigning the object to the empty method.

The _init_() function is a special function and gets called whenever a new object of the corresponding class is instantiated. Functions defined within a body of the class are known as methods and are basic functions. Methods define the behaviors of an object. In Python, polymorphism refers to the ability to use a shared interface for several data types. An illustration is a program that has defined two classes Tilapia and Shark all of which share the method jump() even though they have different functions. By creating common interface jumping_test() we allowed polymorphism in the program above. We then passed objects bonny and biggy in the jumping_test() function.

Part 14: File Management and Exception Handling in Python

File Methods in Python

These methods enable the user to manipulate files in an easy and efficient manner. The methods are preloaded and the user only needs to understand where they can apply.

Directory in Python

Python allows us to arrange several files into different directories for easier handling. The collection of files and subdirectories in Python is known as a directory. The os module in Python contains methods for working with directories.

Getting Current Directory in Python

The keyword getcwd() method is used to get the current working directory. The method will return the current working directory in a string form. The getwcwdb()is also used to get a directory.

Changing Directory

The chdir() method helps modify the existing directory. However, the new path we intend to create should be given a string as a method. The path elements can be separated using the backward slash\ or the forward slash/.

Example

Start IDLE.

Navigate to the File menu and click New Window.

Type the following:

os.chdir('C:\\Tutorial')

print(os.getcwd())

Practice Exercise

Use the chdir() to change a directory in the Python root folder on your computer.

Files and List Directories

The listdir() method in Python is used to determine all files and subdirectories within a directory.

The listdir() method accepts a path and gives a file lists and subdirectories in that particular path. The listdir() will return from the current working directory if no path is specified.

Example

Start IDLE.

Navigate to the File menu and click New Window.

Type the following:

print(os.getcwd())

C:\Tutorial

os.listdir()

os.listdir('D:\\')

Creating a New Directory

The mkdir() method can be used to create a new directory. The method accepts the path of the new directory and will create a new directory in the current working directory in case the particular path is not defined.

os.mkdir('week2')

os.listdir()

File or a Directory Renaming in Python

In Python, the rename()method is used to rename a file or a directory. The old name is given as the argument 1 and the new name is given as argument 2.

Practice Exercise

Create a directory using the Python method and name it Lesson. Rename it using a Python method to Python Lessons.

Removing File or Directory in Python

The remove() method is used to delete a file in Python. Likewise, rmdir() is used to remove an empty directory.

Example

Start IDLE.

Navigate to the File menu and click New Window.

Type the following:

os.listdir()

['mine_direct']

os.rmdir('mine_direct')

Errors and Exceptions

When the Python interpreter encounters errors it will raise exceptions. For instance, dividing a number by zero will lead to an exception.

Example of an Error

Start IDLE.

Navigate to the File menu and click New Window.

Type the following:

if y < 3

  if y < 3

at runtime errors can still occur like when we open a file that does not exist. A file may not exist because it has been renamed and we are accessing using the old name or the file has been deleted. The file could have the same name but has changed the file extension. Python will create an exception object whenever these runtime error types occur.

Inbuilt Exceptions in Python

Python has several inbuilt exceptions that are flagged when associated errors arise. The local() method can help list all inbuilt exceptions in Python.

Exception Handling in Python

If exceptions occur, the execution of a program stops and the exception is passed to the calling process for handling. If the exception is not handled, a program will crash. Thought: Have you tried opening a smartphone app that says "the app has stopped". Can you imagine a program that crashes if it cannot file the image you trying to attach? Exception handling is critical in creating effective programs and also for security. Can you imagine if a hacker realizes that your program will crash and require restarting each time it fails to load an image, the hacker will have a leeway disrupting your software. Fortunately, exception handling allows us to anticipate and give way forward to a program should it encounter an exception.

Handling an Exception by Catching the Exception in Python

Start IDLE.

Navigate to the File menu and click New Window.

Type the following:

import sys

my_list= ['b', 1 ,3]

for entry in my_list:

   try:

```
print("Our entry is", my_entry)

r = 1/int(my_entry)

break

except:

print("Unfortunate",sys.exc_info()[0],"has occured.")

print("Try again.")

print()

print("The reciprocal of the number",my_entry,"is",r)

import sys
```

User Defined Exception

Sometimes a user may need to create own exceptions that best align with your programming needs and these are known as user-defined exceptions.

A user has to create a new class and derive from the class, Exception class.

Summary

Files are used for future storage. To read from a file we need to open it and once through with it, we have to close it to free the resources tied with the file in Python. The inbuilt function open() in Python is used to launch a file. When this function is invoked, a file object is accessed and loaded sometimes referred to as a handle and it is used to modify or read the file accordingly. For the readlines() method, it will scan the entire file lines. After reading the entire file, the reading method will report empty status. The reason for empty status is because there are no more arguments for the method to process. The read() will go through each line in the file till there is no more lines to scan.

The 'r' is used to launch the file for reading and is the default. The 'w' is preferred when launching a file for writing. For exclusive file creation, we use the 'x' mode. The operation will be unsuccessful if the file already we want already exists. The other mode, 'a' is used to launch a file for adding data at the file end while retaining earlier content. The 'a' model will create a new file in case it does not exist. For the 't' mode, it will launch the file in default text mode. The 'b' mode is sued to launch the file in binary mode. Lastly, the '+' mode is used for launching the file to allow reading and writing.

SEVENTH DAY

Part 15: Memoization, Modules, and Packages

This is the method of caching a functional call's results. When you go through and memorize a function, you are only able to evaluate it by looking up the results that you obtained the first time that you had put those parameters to your function.

The log for this is often known as the Memoization cache. In some situations, you are going to find that the lookup failed. This simply means that the function wasn't able to call using those parameters. Only at that time would running your function really be necessary.

Memoization doesn't make much sense unless the function is deterministic, or you can simply accept the result as out of date. But, if your function is expensive, a big speedup would happen when you use this process. Let's back up a bit and see what this all means.

As a programmer, you know that when you do a recursion, it is going to make it easy for you to break up a big problem into pieces that are smaller and more manageable. Try considering iterative sets against the recursive solutions for a Fibonacci sum. Recursive solutions are often simpler when you are reading and then writing a branching problem. You will notice that graph traversals, mathematical series, and tree traversals are often done with recursion. Even though it does offer you a ton of convenience, the computational time that comes with recursion can be very big.

Doing Manual Memoization

The first approach that we are going to use is going to require you to take advantage of a feature out of Python, one that most people are not that excited about, to add state to a function. We can do that with the following code:

```
def fib_default_memoizedn, cache = {}):
if n in cache: ans=cache[n]
elif n<= 2:ans =1
cache[n]=ans else:
ans=fib_default_memoized(n-2)+fib_default_memoized(n-1)
cache[n]=ans
```

RETURN ANS

The basic logic that comes with this is pretty obvious. The
cache is going to be the results dictionary of your previous
calls to the fib_default_memoized(). The 'n' parameter is the
key. It is going to be the nth Fibonacci number. If this is true,
then you are done. But if it is not true, then you have to take
the time to evaluate this as the version of the native recursive
and keep it in the cache before the return of the results.

The thing here is 'cache' is the function's keyword parameter.
Python is usually going to evaluate the keyword parameters only
one time, which is when you import the function. This means
that if there are any issues with mutability in your
parameter, it is only going to be initialized one time. This is
usually the basis of small bugs that happen in the program, but
in this case, you are going to mutate your parameter in order to
take advantage of it.

Manual Memoization: Objects

Some programmers who use Python argue that going through and mutating your formal parameters is a bad idea. For others, especially those who like to work with Java, the argument for this is that all functions that have state need to be turned into objects. An example of how this would look like in your compiler includes the following: class Fib():

```
CACHE = {}
```

```
DEF__CALL__(SELF, n):
if n in self.cache: ans = self.cache[n] if n <= 2:
ans = 1 self.cache[n] = ans else:
ans = self(n-2) + self(n -1) self.cache[n] = ans
```

RETURN ANS

If you are doing this one, the call dunder method is going to be used to make the Fib instances behave like a function. The Cache is shared by all the Fib instances because that is its class attribute. When you are looking at Fibonacci numbers, this is a desirable thing to do. However, if your object made calls to a server well defined in the constructor, and the result was going to depend on the server, this may not be a good thing. Instead, you would need to move it over to an object attribute by taking it right to the 'init' part. Either way, you will get the speed up process from this.

Manual Memoization: Using 'Global"

Another thing that we can work on with this process is manual memoization with the help of the 'Global' function. You can go through and evade your default parameters and some of the hacky mutations simply by adding in 'global'. This is one thing that sometimes gets a bad reputation with programmers, but it is a good one to learn how to use. Many times you would use the global here declaration because it works better, but you would use the same kind of coding that we had above.

Decorators

The last thing we are going to talk about here is a decorator. This is simply a higher order function. What this means is that the function is going to be the argument and then it will return to you another function. When it comes to these decorators, the returned function is going to usually be the original function, which has been augmented to be more functional. An example of this would be to make decorate that is going to allow you to print text each time a function is called. The way that you can write this out is:

def output_decorator(f): def f_(f)

f()

*print('Ran f...') return f_*

You can take the decorated version to replace the f. You just need to do 'F=output_decorator(f)'. Just by calling the f(), you are going to get your decorated version. Python is going to make this even easier if you just use the following syntax to help.

@output_decorator def f()
#...define f...

Now, if you go through and try to do this, you will find that the result from the output_decortor is not that motivating. But you can go beyond this and augment the operation of the function itself. For example, you could include a type of cache with the decorator and then intercept the calls to the function if needed.

But if you try to write out your own decorator, there are times when you get confused in the particulars of the argument passing, and then getting really stuck with the introspection of Python when you figure this out. Introspection is the capacity to determine when you run the program, the type of an object. This is one of the strengths of the Python language, but if you are using a decorator, things can become messy.

If you are going to use one of the decorators, be careful with what you are doing here. You want to make sure that you understand how to make them work and that you actually need to use it in your code. Otherwise, you may run into some issues with the code, and it may not interpret in the compiler the right way.

Python Modules

Modules consist of definitions as well as program statements. An illustration is a file name config.py which is considered as a module. The module name would be config. Modules are sued to help break large programs into smaller manageable and organized files as well as promoting reusability of code.

Example

Creating the First module

Start IDLE.

Navigate to the File menu and click New Window.

Type the following:

Def add(x, y):

""""This is a program to add two

numbers and return the outcome"""

outcome=x+y

return outcome

Module Import

The keyword import is used to import.

Example

Import first

The dot operator can help us access a function as long as we know the name of the module.

Example

Start IDLE.

Navigate to the File menu and click New Window.

Type the following:

first.add(6,8)

Import Statement in Python

The import statement can be used to access the definitions within a module via the dot operator.

Start IDLE.

Navigate to the File menu and click New Window.

Type the following:

import math

print("The PI value is", math.pi)

Import with renaming

Example

Start IDLE.

Navigate to the File menu and click New Window.

Type the following:

import math as h

  print("The PI value is-",h.pi)

Discussion

In this case, h is our renamed math module with a view helping save typing time in some instances. When we rename the new name becomes valid and recognized one and not the original one.

From...import statement Python.

It is possible to import particular names from a module rather than importing the entire module.

Example

Start IDLE.

Navigate to the File menu and click New Window.

Type the following:

from math import pi

print("The PI value is-", pi)

Importing All Names

Example

Start IDLE.

Navigate to the File menu and click New Window.

Type the following:

from math import*

print("The PI value is-", pi)

Discussion

In this context, we are importing all definitions from a particular module but it is encouraged norm as it can lead to unseen duplicates.

Module Search Path in Python

Example

Start IDLE.

Navigate to the File menu and click New Window.

Type the following:

import sys

sys.path

Python searches everywhere including the sys file.

Reloading a Module

Python will only import a module once increasing efficiency in execution.

print("This program was executed")

import mine

Reloading Code

Example

Start IDLE.

Navigate to the File menu and click New Window.

Type the following:

import mine

import mine

import mine

mine.reload(mine)

Dir() Built-In Python function

For discovering names contained in a module, we use the dir() inbuilt function.

Syntax

dir(module_name)

Python Package

Files in python hold modules and directories are stored in packages. A single package in Python holds similar modules. Therefore, different modules should be placed in different Python packages.

Summary

A module is a Python object with arbitrarily named attributes that you can bind and reference. Simply, a module is a file consisting of Python code. A module can define functions, classes and variables. A module can also include runnable code. A package is a collection of Python modules: while a module is a single Python file, a package is a directory of Python modules containing an additional __init__.py file, to distinguish a package from a directory that just happens to contain a bunch of Python scripts.

Part 16: Time and Date

The module datetime in Python enables us to work with times and dates.

Getting Current Time and Date

```
import datetime
datetime_today=datetime.datetime.now()
print(datetime_today)                    #Will return the current time and date
```

Discussion

We imported the datetime module using the import datetime statement. The datetime class is defined in the datetime module. The now() method is invoked to create a datetime object containing the local date and time now.

Example

```
import datetime
date_today=datetime.date.today()
print(date_today)
```

Discussion

In this program we used the today() method specified in the date class to extract date object.

Understanding the Datetime Module

Python allows us to use the dir() function to extract a list containing all attributes of a module.

Example

```
import datetime
print(dir(datetime))
```

The commonly used classes in the datetime module include date Class, time Class, datetime Class, and timedelta Class among others.

Date Object

import datetime

t = datetime.date(2018, 5, 6)

print(t)

Discussion

The date() in the example is a constructor of the date class and the constructor accepts three arguments: year, month and day.

Example 2

from datetime import date

b=date(2018,5,6)

print(b)

Practice Exercise

- ✓ In example 2 explain what is b
- ✓ Explain the statement 'from datetime import date'.

Example 3

Using the today() class method we can create a date object containing the current date.

```
from datetime import date

day = date.today()

print("Date today =", today)
```

Timestamp

It is also possible to create date objects from a time stamp. The fromtimestamp() method we can create a current date object.

Example

```
from datetime import date
timetoday = date.fromtimestamp(1235153363)
print("Date =", timetiday)
```

Printing Current Date

Example

```
from datetime import date

timetoday = date.timetoday()

print("Current year:", timetoday.year)
print("Current month:",timetoday.month)
print("Current day:", timetoday.day)
```

Time Object

The local time is a time object instantiated from the time class.

Example

```
from datetime import time

m = time()
print("m =", m)

n = time(11, 34, 56)
print("n =", n)

p = time(hour = 11, minute = 34, second = 56)
print("p =", p)

f = time(11, 34, 56, 234566)
print("f =", f)
```

Print Hour to Microsecond

Example

```
from datetime import time

m = time(11, 34, 56)

print("hour =", m.hour)
print("minute =", m.minute)
print("second =", m.second)
print("microsecond =", m.microsecond)
```

Datetime Object

Example

```
from datetime import datetime

m = datetime(2019, 1, 15)
print(m)

n = datetime(2018, 10, 27, 22, 56, 58, 351270)
print(n)
```

Discussion

The datetime() constructor takes three arguments year, month and day.

Print Year to the Minute

Example

```python
from datetime import datetime

m = datetime(2018, 10, 27, 25, 54, 53, 351270)
print("year =", m.year)
print("month =", m.month)
print("hour =", m.hour)
print("minute =", m.minute)
print("timestamp =", m.timestamp())
```

Using Timedelta

In Python, a timedelta object represents the difference between two times or dates.

```python
from datetime import datetime, date

time1 = date(year = 2019, month = 1, day = 12)
time2 = date(year = 2018, month = 11, day = 22)
time3 = time1 - time2
print("time3 =", time3)

time4 = datetime(year = 2018, month = 7, day = 12, hour = 7, minute = 9, second = 33)
time5 = datetime(year = 2019, month = 6, day = 10, hour = 5, minute = 55, second = 13)
time6 = time4 - time5
print("time6 =", time6)

print("type of time3 =", type(time3))
print("type of time6 =", type(time6))
```

Getting Difference Between Two Timedelta Objects

```
from datetime import timedelta

time1 = timedelta(weeks = 4, days = 10, hours = 2, seconds = 56)
time2 = timedelta(days = 6, hours = 11, minutes = 8, seconds = 34)
time3 = time1 - time2

print("time3 =", time3)
```

Discussion

In this program, we created timedelta objects time1 and time2 and their difference displayed on the screen.

From Datetime Import Timedelta

```
time1 = timedelta(seconds = 33)
time2 = timedelta(seconds = 54)
time3 = time1 - time2

print("time3 =", time3)
print("time3 =", abs(time3))
```

Duration in Seconds

```
from datetime import timedelta

time = timedelta(days = 4, hours = 2, seconds = 56, microseconds = 31423)
print("total seconds =", time.total_seconds())
```

NOTE

In Python one can find the sum of two times and date using the + operator. It is also to divide and multiply a timedelta object by floats and integers.

Format Datetime in Python

Formatting datetime attributes are achieved through strftime() and strptime() methods. In Python the strftime() method is specified under classes datetime, date and time.

Using the method will format a string from a given datetime, date or time object.

Example

```python
from datetime import datetime

now = datetime.now()

time = now.strftime("%H:%M:%S")
print("time:", time)

string1 = now.strftime("%m/%d/%Y, %H:%M:%S")
print("string1:", string1)

string2 = now.strftime("%d/%m/%Y, %H:%M:%S")
# dd/mm/YY H:M:S format
print("string2:", string2)
```

Discussion

In this program, the following are format codes %m, %Y,%H, and %d and the strftime() method accepts one or more format codes and a gives a formatted string. In the program, time, string1, and string2 are strings.

From strptime() to datetime

In Python, the strptime () will create a datetime object from a specified string that represents date and time.

Example

```
from datetime import datetime

date_mine = "15 March, 2017"
print("date_mine =", date_mine)

object_date = datetime.strptime(object_date, "%d %B, %Y")
print("object_date =", object_date)

Discussion
In Python, the strptime() accepts two arguments namely a string capturing date and time, and format code
Timezone in Python
A third party module pytZ is recommended for handling timezone needs in Python.
from datetime import datetime
import pytz
local = datetime.now()
print("Local:", local.strftime("%m/%d/%Y, %H:%M:%S"))
Mumbai_tz = pytz.timezone('Asia/India')
datetime_Mumbai = datetime.now(Mumbai_tz)
print("NY:", datetime_Mumbai.strftime("%m/%d/%Y, %H:%M:%S"))
Lagos_tz = pytz.timezone('Africa/Lagos')
datetime_Lagos = datetime.now(Lagos_tz)
print("Lagos:", datetime_Lagos.strftime("%m/%d/%Y, %H:%M:%S"))
```

Discussion

In this program, the Mumbai_tz and Lagos_tz are datetime objects holding current time and date of their corresponding timezone

Summary

Example: Python get today's date.

Here, we imported date class from the datetime module. Then, we used date.today() method to get the current local date. By the way, today variable will be a date object. You can use strftime() method to create string representing date in different formats from this object.

Conclusion

Thank you for making it through to the end of this book. I hope it was informative and able to provide you with all of the tools you need to achieve your goals whatever they may be.

The next step is to take a look at some of the topics and the things that we discuss in this book, and put them to use. There are many different things that you will be able to do with the Python language, and this book aimed to help you get started with a few of the more complex parts that you may want to add into your code.

When you are done, you will be able to combine this information with your basics and make some really powerful codes.

When you have spent some time working on the Python language and you are ready to take your skills to the next level and develop some strong codes that can do so much in just a few lines, make sure to read through this book to help you get started!